150 Years
Up North and More

Copyright © 2018 Latitude 46 Publishing
No part of this book may be reproduced or transmitted in any form by any means, except for brief passages quoted by a reviewer, without written permission from the publisher or, in the case of photography, a license from Access ©: the Canadian Copyright Licensing Agency.

Library and Archives Canada Cataloguing in Publication

150 years up north and more / Karen McCauley and Laura Stradiotto, editors.

ISBN 978-0-9958235-9-4 (softcover)

1. Creative nonfiction, Canadian (English)--Ontario, Northern. I. McCauley, Karen, 1968-, editor II. Stradiotto, Laura, 1978-, editor III. **Title: One hundred fifty years up north and more.**

PS8255.O5A15 2018   C814'.608097131   C2018-901292-7

Book design: Christine Lewis
Cover artwork: Sarah King Gold

Published by Latitude 46 Publishing

109 Elm Street, Suite 205
Sudbury, Ontario P3C 1T4
info@latitude46publishing.com
www.latitude46publishing.com

We acknowledge the support of the Canada Council for the Arts, which last year invested $153 million to bring the arts to Canadians throughout the country.

Nous remercions le Conseil des arts du Canada de son soutien. L'an dernier, le Conseil a investi 153 millions de dollars pour mettre de l'art dans la vie des Canadiennes et des Canadiens de tout le pays.

150 Years
Up North and More

Karen McCauley and Laura Stradiotto, editors

Introduction

In recognition of Canada's 150th birthday, we set out to publish an anthology of Creative Non-Fiction stories to recognize the many experiences that have formed the diverse and multicultural part of Ontario; both the Anishinaabe who witnessed the influx of immigrants to their territory and newcomers who left familiarity of home and loved ones in search for a better life.

Once we started reading submissions, we were struck by how they speak to important contemporary conversations that we are having about issues pertaining to globalization, migration, reconciliation; large concepts that are perhaps best illustrated through stories of individual journeys.

These journeys may entail crossing oceans, or be contained within a small geographical space that has always been home to the storyteller, and to the storyteller's ancestors for longer than time is measured. Through these diverse and moving narratives, the reader learns that "home" is a complex idea; something that many people give their entire lives to defending or seeking.

We are thankful to all the authors who have generously shared their personal stories of life *Up North*. The literature contained within the pages of this book speaks to our collective experience as northern Ontario residents; it defines our past, reflects our present and will ultimately shape our future.

– Editors Karen McCauley and Laura Stradiotto

Table of Contents

Muriel's Medicine, Margo Little 1
From Serra Bruno...to Sudbury,
Franca Dominelli Lisi 15
On Being Francophone, Julie-Anne Bolduc 28
Her Woven Memory, Kim Fahner 36
My Story, Hussein Qarqouz 43
Adrift, Liisa Kovala 46
We Are the Undesirables, Julio Heleno Gomes 57
History of Small Handed Women,
Susan Eldridge-Vautour 72
A Minnow Catcher, Caitlin Sylvia McAuliffe 79
Identity Confessions, William Morin 93
The Original Hard Woman, Shawna Diane Partridge 102
A Farewell to Steam, Rod Carley 114
Literacy, Alfred Fitzpatrick and My Vocation in Algoma,
Evelyn Clara Diebel 133
Living with Grandmother, Lee Weimer 142
The Hotel, Sarah McComb 151
The Newcomers, Rosanna Micelotta Battigelli 163
Waiting for the Ice to Melt, Darlene Naponse 174
Acknowledgements 183
Contributor biographies 184
Editor biographies 191

Muriel's Medicine: A Memoir
By Margo Little

Truth

During my childhood on Manitoulin Island, segregation was the norm and racial stereotypes were firmly entrenched. Most communities were governed by strict religious dictates and a rigid class system that had been imported from overseas. If a Catholic woman consented to marry a Protestant man, for instance, the union would invite ostracism. Similarly, if a European man married an Indigenous woman they were often shunned. On Western Manitoulin in the mid-Twentieth Century white settlers endured a hardscrabble existence on inhospitable acreages while their Indigenous neighbours were relegated to small remote parcels of land known as reserves.

My mother's ancestors were based in West Bay, now known as M'Chigeeng First Nation. According to the Office of the Indian Registrar in Ottawa, my great-grandfather opted for voluntary enfranchisement in 1921, which involved surrender of land in favour of the right to vote. Giving up your status was supposed to bring advantages but it brought only conflict with other band members and years of struggle. Eventually, my great grandparents moved to Wisconsin, but my grandfather married an island girl and settled in Mindemoya in Central Manitoulin. The six children they raised, including my mother, were assimilated into mainstream society and encouraged to hide their Indigenous roots. Even the names on birth certificates were altered in a small but significant way to distinguish the new branch of the family from the relatives on reserve. When my mother married an Irish trapper/farmer in 1946, all references to Native background ceased.

But no matter how people try to suppress their heritage for the sake of survival or for the sake of their children, there's always a segment of the settler population that harbours a long memory and a deep-seated desire to discourage mixing races or religions or cultures.

This is the story about my own first-hand encounter with prejudice as a mixed race child and about the advent of a gentle healer who entered my life at a particularly traumatic time. In our short time together in 1956 she shared seven guiding principles that steer my life to this day. And for that I am eternally grateful.

Bravery

"You squaw; you dirty squaw! Why don't you go back to the reservation where you belong?" The hateful voices came from somewhere near the school flag pole, but I didn't dare raise my eyes, didn't dare react to the comments. It would only provoke more attacks.

The stinging words had strafed me from the moment I started first grade at the rural school. At first, it didn't seem possible that they were talking to me; I was blissfully unaware that I was considered an Indian, but day after day the taunting persisted. The bullies had found an easy target. I was learning the hard way that my high cheek bones and distinctive features were not acceptable.

When the bell finally rang, I scurried to the refuge of the one-room school house. The township troublemakers followed close behind. The teacher never let on that she heard the others picking on me. She was young and vulnerable in her first teaching job; she had enough problems protecting herself from the ruffians. Was she intimidated by them too or did she just not care about the persecution? I never knew. Most of my days unfolded in this tense way. The routine did not vary.

Bigger girls would make fun of my clothes. Bigger boys would follow me and grope me when they thought no one was looking. The intent was to shame and humiliate the newcomer. But there were worse things to come. My world was about to be turned upside down in a new way.

One fall afternoon, just after I had opened my English composition book, my paternal grandfather appeared unexpectedly at the door. Twisting a sweat-soiled cap in his hands, he spoke in hushed tones to the teacher. At first I couldn't make out the words, but then I heard "pneumonia" and "Sick Kids Hospital." The few muffled phrases made my heart tremble; I knew my parents had taken an emergency trip to Toronto and now I was certain that something terrible had happened to Greg. Since birth, my five-year-old brother had been afflicted with a severe curvature of the spine and had suffered from all the painful complications that accompany such a hereditary defect.

In an unaccustomed display of warmth, my grandfather clutched my small brown hand in his large callused white one. He didn't let go as he led me to the old pick-up truck by the road. All the way back to the farm he was ominously silent.

The next thing I can remember is the cramped parlour at the old farm house filled with baskets of white lilies and neighbours funneling solemnly past a small coffin.

Seemingly invisible to the adults, I received no explanation of Greg's passing, nor was I comforted in any way. I stared at the unfamiliar rituals, with strangers coming and going, and I found myself quite forgotten. In those times a child's need to grieve was seldom acknowledged. The grown-ups spoke in whispers and looked past me when I reached out for solace, for any kind of reassurance.

Mother retreated into seclusion in the days that followed the burial. Through my adult lens I can now perceive that she was physically and mentally depleted from labouring on the farm and travelling to Toronto for doctor appointments. Sometimes I could hear her crying in the middle of the night and I yearned to go to her. But instead I dried my own tears and tried to make sense of the deep freeze that had descended upon the world. As for father, he went away to work in the timber camps up north. Mother's two sisters came from Mindemoya to help out temporarily. But when I looked for guidance from the aunties, I was scolded. In a chorus of disapproval they chided me; "leave your mother alone; can't you see she's been through enough?"

For me, both home and school had become unbearable. There was no relief in either place. Since I had always watched over Greg and served as his guardian, I was now completely lost.

I didn't know it at the time, but my prayers would be answered in an unusual way. A new force for good was about to enter my life.

Love

One day after school, I was sobbing inconsolably by the woodpile when I sensed a shadowy presence nearby. I remember squinting upwards to see a slim, brown-skinned young woman with a prominent nose and long black hair. She was staring intently at me and manipulating a wad of chewing tobacco in her protruding lower lip.

"Here, I brought you some Kool Aid," the stranger said, handing me a metal cup. "Will you show me where you keep the milk buckets?"

The Good Samaritan, who appeared by my side during those dark times, turned out to be "the hired girl" father had dispatched to work on the farm while he was away logging. The aunties couldn't stay much longer; they had families of their own to take care of and mother had taken to bed, unable to face her burden of sorrow.

In retrospect, I can only imagine the depth of my mother's depression after Greg's death. She had always been an energetic, athletic woman with a biting sense of humour. She came from a large, impoverished family on Central Manitoulin and was forced to drop out of school in grade nine to work; after marriage she was even more dirt poor. For this outgoing, vibrant young woman, the isolation and hardships of farm life on Western Manitoulin must have been stultifying. Looking back, I realize it was a survival tactic to deny her Indigenous heritage. Naturally, to have her second child, her only son, taken at the age of five was a devastating blow.

She was unable to be there for me in those days of bereavement. I learned to fend for myself and to hang around with Muriel, our hired helper.

Muriel was strong and agile while forking hay, hoisting milk cans and pitching manure. I was fascinated by the aloof, matter-of-fact way my new-found companion went about the mundane tasks of the farm. She was short on conversation, but often grinned amiably in my direction.

At school, however, the unprovoked nastiness continued. The hulking farm boys from the township would gather around me in manure-covered boots to torture me unmercifully. "Squaw; filthy wagon burner!" they'd spit at me. Following the teacher's model, I turned the other cheek and escaped into reading books and using my imagination to create an alternate reality. No point in aggravating my mother's misery by asking for help with the abusers. All the while I missed Greg desperately. It was painful enough to lose my beloved baby brother but now it seemed that my parents had abandoned me too.

Humility

One particularly lonely evening, I found myself drawn to Muriel's room where Johnny Cash, our favourite singer, was belting out a vinyl tune on a scratchy record player. With the music blaring, our boarder motioned me to step inside.

Scanning the room, I noticed the sparse personal effects Muriel had brought with her from the Sheshegwaning reserve. She was sitting cross-legged on a low bed, rolling cigarettes with Zig Zag papers and a pouch of Amphora tobacco. On her rickety orange crate dresser sat a series of birch bark scoops and trays held together with balsam gum. One container held a can of Copenhagen snuff and another bulged with a pile of 45s featuring the legendary "Man in Black." Matches were stored in a simple birch bark dish reinforced with slippery elm and edged with sweet-grass.

"Who's that?" I asked boldly, pointing to a black and white photograph she had displayed on the window sill.

Muriel licked the flap of the rolling paper and tucked the tobacco in tight before she replied. "That's my girl," she said shyly. "She's just about your age; she's away at school right now, with the nuns. I miss her a lot but I hope she can come home for a visit."

For a moment, I stared at the picture of the other young girl; she too was separated from her mother and learning to cope on her own. For a moment, my isolation was eased. Something about Muriel's manner invited me to unleash all the questions that I had been suppressing. Bursting with the weight of unanswered riddles about life and death, I had found someone willing to listen. And in her unique unhurried and understated way, my older friend responded to my unfulfilled mother-hunger.

Naturally attuned to a young girl's confusion, Muriel gradually introduced me to the teachings that she relied upon to survive. She began by telling me about the four stages of life and the gifts of the four directions, about the old ways my own mother had left behind.

"Your brother was taken in the first stage of life," she said quietly. "It is only natural for you to feel sad and helpless. In the past, our ancestors would have placed Greg on a platform with his feet toward the West; they would have waited four days for his spirit to leave his body and go to the Land of Souls. And they would have kept a small fire burning to light his path there. In that way you would have been able to let him go; I think maybe you feel bad that Greg had to go there on his own."

I remember drinking in the comforting words and feeling my terror begin to subside in the days that followed. I felt somehow relieved and soothed by the words from my surrogate mother.

Respect

Muriel's lessons were seamlessly woven into our daily chores on the farm. As always, the labour and demands of rural life escalated in the spring. After school we would travel an old bush road to the back acreage where the milk cows grazed during the day. On these trips I would often flinch when I heard twigs snapping in the underbrush. Unidentified noises overhead made me skittish. Muriel would listen and observe calmly, but I was anxious if a fox crossed our path or bear droppings were visible on the road.

Muriel always stopped during our journeys to set my mind at ease with a new installment in her storytelling. "The animals are our fellow travellers on Mother Earth; we need to honour them as our friends," she said. "We look to them for our clothing, our food and our tools; we look to them to tell us about the seasons and the weather; you will see; there's nothing to be scared of."

And then she'd laugh and tease the blue jay for being so raucous in a nearby tree. At other times she'd caution me to be still to watch a woodpecker hammering on a dead stump. This behaviour she would interpret as a warning of a thunderstorm as she dashed down the trail ahead of me. Walks with Muriel were never predictable.

Honesty

Most days we were inseparable, but then one Sunday afternoon Muriel was nowhere to be found. I had searched the barn, the chicken coop and the outhouse, but my confidante had vanished. Finally, I remembered the pond next to a neighbouring farm. I raced across the field to the small man-made watering hole we had visited a few days earlier.

Muriel was indeed there. She was hunched under a silver birch tree, her tobacco smoke curling in the air. As I shyly approached, she moved a little to give me some room on the blanket.

"I looked all over for you," I gasped, short of breath after the recent exertion. "Why didn't you say where you were going?"

Muriel extinguished her half-finished cigarette on a stone. "It's my moon time now," she confided. "And I like to get away by myself for awhile."

"Moon time," I repeated with a quizzical expression. "What's that? Do you mean you're going crazy?"

This comment brought the heartiest laugh I had ever heard from my mentor. "No, silly, I'm not loony," Muriel answered. "It just means I am having my monthly period. It might be something you want to talk to your Mom about."

"Maybe," I said, dropping my gaze. "I've heard the grade eight girls whisper about it at school. Diane and Barbara have already started theirs."

Muriel shifted her lean body on the blanket and allowed her eyes to follow the path of two geese circling to alight on the pond. "Should I leave then?" I asked, looking for signs of rejection in the older woman's face.

"No, you can stay," Muriel smiled. "Traditions have changed a lot for us over time. When I was little, it wasn't unusual for us to go to a little moon hut in the bush for days, even a month sometimes."

"That must have been really scary," I responded, brown eyes wide. "Imagine being all by yourself in the bush...."

"It might seem that way," Muriel agreed. "But being on your own for a while can be a good thing. A long time ago our people would have sent a girl off into the bush to fast and to think about what it means to be a woman. She would be told to expect a visit from her spirit helper. This guardian spirit would come to her only after she had gone through great sorrow and suffering. If a girl received a vision, she would be doubly blessed."

"And how do you know when you're ready?" I asked.

"You must be patient and you will know when it is the right moment," Muriel said. "The dark clouds will part and your path will be made clear. Only you can know what feels right for you."

After the Sunday revelations by the pond I found myself day-dreaming frequently. My mind wandered from my lessons at school, from my chores on the farm. I was lost in repetitive thoughts of Greg. Why was he taken in the first stage of life? He would never have a chance to grow up, to enjoy all the bounties of the Earth. The Creator had sent him on his journey to the West early and my little brother had disappeared over the edge of the world.

In dreams I followed his tracks as he got closer to the Land of Souls. I witnessed him approaching a treacherous bridge suspended over white water below. Greg cried out in fear as he tried to balance on the slippery logs and his screams were lost in the wailing wind.

9

Before he could secure his footing, the bridge was transformed into a gigantic water snake flailing about and threatening to fling him into the abyss.

Worry about my brother and heartache over the virtual absence of my parents finally sapped all my strength. A tenacious cold and cough settled in my lungs and throat rendering my body lethargic and heavy. With mother still reclusive and depressed I resolved to endure the illness without complaint.

Muriel watched from the sidelines for a few days before intervening with her own cure. I came downstairs to the kitchen one morning to find her crushing strips of spruce bark; these she boiled on the wood stove until the room was musty with the medicinal smell. With initial reluctance I accepted the steaming cup and began to sip the solution. Later, with trust growing in natural healing remedies, I showed Muriel a small cut on my finger. With maternal compassion she gently placed warm spruce gum on a cloth and applied it to my wound.

Forever afterwards I would associate the aroma of spruce and wintergreen with Muriel's sojourn at the farm. When the cold had released its grip, we spent time weeding the garden and Muriel shared more innate knowledge about the healing powers of plants.

"Every plant has a place and a purpose designed by the Creator," she said. "Sometimes the gift of a certain root or herb will come to you in a dream. You must thank the Creator and the plant for giving us beauty and medicine."

If truth be told, I was not entirely convinced about the efficacious nature of some of the stubborn vegetation on our farm. I most likely grimaced as I yanked pigweed and burdock from the rows of carrots and potatoes.

"But, of course," Muriel said, with a meaningful glance, "Natural problems need natural cures; sickness of the spirit needs a supernatural cure."

As I continued to struggle with childhood loss, and to search for meaning in all that had transpired, I often sensed that nothing could be hidden from my counselor. With her penetrating brown eyes, Muriel took in everything.

I needed time to ponder Muriel's esoteric comments, but soon school was out and summer beckoned. With warm weather and freedom from schoolyard harassment, my vitality returned. During previous summer breaks, our family had enjoyed games and picnics at the Huron shores or car rides to visit grandparents in Mindemoya and Tehkummah. This year, however, such outings were too painful without Greg. Mother's fragile emotional condition coupled with father's absence meant everyone would stick close to home.

In July, I accompanied Muriel on a strawberry picking expedition behind the old gravel pit near the farm. The sun-baked berries tumbled willingly with the mere touch of our nimble brown hands. Muriel showed me how to make a scoop container out of birch bark to hold the berries once the tin lard pails were overflowing.

As she, herself, had been instructed by her grandmother, Muriel selected a dignified birch tree and began to gather bark for her crafts. Before cutting a vertical incision in the tree, Muriel taught me to thank the spirit of the woods for protection and good will. She offered tobacco to the sky, to the earth, and then she placed tobacco at the foot of the tree. "Miigwetch, Father Sun, Mother Earth," she prayed.

As Muriel harvested the strips, she paused with her hand respectfully on the tree. "You know," she said, "The elders say they used to wrap layers of birch bark around the bodies of those who died; it preserved them until their spirit could take its leave and make its journey."

I did not reply immediately. I was too preoccupied by the stark images of dead bodies enveloped in shrouds of tissue paper thin birch bark. I couldn't help but wonder if Greg would have liked that idea. I wondered if he had made it to the Land of Souls without the fire to guide him. And I wondered if mother would ever hug me again. Would father ever come home again?

August brought cooler weather. Muriel had gone home to Sheshegwaning to see her daughter for a few days. I shouldered the chores alone but I didn't mind. Although mother was beginning to be a little more approachable, a little less isolated, I was careful not to push. As was her custom, Muriel had coached me to be patient. "One day soon your mother's spirit will reawaken. I promise," she whispered as she departed.

One day, near summer's end, I set out as usual for the back fields to round up the cows for milking. On the return trip I shivered as the sky darkened and a fierce thunderstorm rolled in. To my dismay, the lead cow bolted at the first clap of thunder; with her tail held straight in the air, she disappeared in the trees. The panic was contagious as the rest of the herd stampeded after her.

A few sprinkles of rain fell and chain lightning seared the sky. I automatically sprinted in the direction of the lead cow's bell and fought my way through the underbrush in a frantic attempt to regroup the spooked Holsteins. After stumbling for several minutes, I stopped to listen. The tinkle of the bell faded; all around me the forest was closing in, but Muriel was not there to guide me home.

Alert to every sound, my imagination leapt to conjure danger behind every conifer and in the call of every bird. The more I struggled to find the main road, the more lost and disoriented I became.

As darkness fell, new night noises made me twitch and jump. But I was determined not to let hysteria defeat my survival instincts. Fighting fatigue and tears, I gathered a pile of cedar boughs and made myself a makeshift bed the way Muriel had demonstrated. As I curled into the green, aromatic nesting place, the comforting words of my friend sustained me: "Courage is fear that has said its prayers."

I clung to Muriel's mantra as I tried to ignore hunger pangs and lull myself to sleep. All sense of time was lost in the darkness; a tiny sliver of a moon and a scattering of cold stars gave sparse illumination to the threatening woods. In this hyper-vigilant state, I succumbed to fitful sleep.

Dawn brought the longed for, yet feared, supernatural visitation. In the half light of the forest, a compelling voice spoke to me in a tone that seemed foreign and yet familiar. Out of the gloom a shadowy figure approached and I recognized the image of Everlasting Standing Woman, as Muriel had once described her.

"Come with me," the ghostly helper invited, as I placed my small brown hand in my guardian's ethereal one. Slowly, we ascended the shining trail that lay before us. Soon the spirit woman stepped away and I became aware of another entity close by. My heart was soothed by his words.

"I have found my way, big sister," Greg said softly. "Thank you for showing me; go now and don't be sad, don't cry. I am home."

Wisdom

Blinding sunlight and blaring car horns broke the connection with the spirit world. I closed my eyes one last time in an attempt to recover the dream and the message of hope, but Greg was beyond reach.

I pushed the cedar boughs aside, and shielding my eyes, set off running in the direction of the search party. Within moments I had emerged from the dark bush to be reunited with anxious but open arms. I savoured the bittersweet emotion of mother embracing me with hugs and reprimands simultaneously. "I was afraid you were lost forever; I can't bear to lose you too," she kept sobbing.

Back in the farm kitchen my mother welcomed me home by peeling a fresh orange and serving hot buttered scones for lunch. Basking in the newly rekindled warmth of mother's love, I reveled in the attention. As Muriel had predicted, the bond severed by grief was finally mended.

My world would never be the same after the vision in the woods. Muriel disappeared from my life as mysteriously as she had entered it; she was never to return to the farm. Instead father left the lumber camp unexpectedly to resume his role. There was a new peacefulness in the house that bolstered my spirit. Now for the first time since Greg's passing, I was not invisible; my parents were letting me know in many ways that I was precious to them. Greg would never be coming back, I accepted, but somehow I felt consoled.

When I look back with an adult's intellect, I realize that many of Muriel's prophecies had come to pass. In the schoolyard the malicious taunting miraculously ceased. And we had another new teacher; one who stood up for herself and for us. I knew then that Muriel's medicine was strong; it was called love.

From Serra San Bruno . . . to Sudbury
By Franca Dominelli Lisi

July 1953. With her heart in her throat, her tears, fears, and good-byes—*Addio e buona fortuna*—to everyone and everything my mother knew and loved, she gathered us up and we left our beloved town of Serra San Bruno, Calabria to immigrate to Canada. I was five years old.

I was born in a town nestled in the mountains of Calabria in southern Italy after my father came back from the Second World War. He had been stationed in Libya. I was my family's third girl, but my father was so happy to be back in one healthy piece that he did not care that I was a girl and not a boy. In Italy, everyone wanted boys. My mother would often tell me that my father would carry me around on top of his shoulders and show me off to anyone that he met along the way. I called my father *papà* and my mother, *mamma*.

My father was always looking for work. As he went about town with me he took every opportunity to talk to different people who could help him secure a day or two of work. The years after the war were very hard. The economy was at an all-time low, and our neighbours and everyone we knew struggled to feed themselves and their families. Like thousands of other Italians, this dire situation propelled my father and his brother to make the decision to immigrate. Few people left their homeland and people they loved willingly. But they came to Canada with hopes and dreams for the possibility of a better life for themselves and their children, which meant finding work so that they wouldn't have to worry about where the next meal was coming from.

Canada needed people for all kinds of trades and work. Canada was willing to let people other than your relatives "sponsor" you; that is, help to bring you over, provide housing, and help you secure a job. My father and uncle were sponsored by a man named Mr. Bonazza, who was related to my uncle. He had come to Canada many years before and was raising his family on his own. His wife had passed away.

I was two years old when my father, Salvatore, and his brother left for Canada in 1950. From Halifax, they journeyed west to Kearney, Ontario to *Signore* Bonazza's house. Kearney was a village in the Muskoka area near Huntsville, with a population of around 300 people. Mr Bonazza owned a large home and had lots of room to accommodate other tenants. He was just like 'Mr. Mom,' making meals and cleaning, and tending to any of their particular needs.

Father and his brother went to work at a coal factory. They were to stay there for a period of two years, after which they would be free to move anywhere they wanted to go or work. My father and uncle chose to stay on at the coal plant.

By 1953 my father had scraped together enough money to be able to bring my mother Rosina and the rest of the family over to Canada. We were four: Sara, fourteen; Virginia, twelve; me (Franca), five; and Bruno, four. Father had also arranged for his father-in-law (our *Nonno* Nicola) to join us. Times were still very hard and my mother had to sell some of her furniture to pay for the boat trip to Canada.

This was a sad and happy time for my mother. She was happy to come to Canada with her children to reunite her family, but she was heartbroken and worried because she had to leave her poor old father in Italy. He had decided that he was too set in his ways to be making the long trip to Canada.

Nonno Nicola was sad to see us leave, but said that we had to go to our new life and be a family again. Years earlier when my mother was young, *Nonno* had lived in the U.S. for seven years. Then he had gone back home to Italy, because his wife, my *Nonna*, had been too afraid to make the boat trip to America.

My father knew, and imagined, how my mother would have felt, which was why when he was preparing for the family to come to Canada, he had also included *Nonno*.

Our house in Serra San Bruno was attached to *Nonno's* house. You walked in and the cement floor was grey and smooth. To the left we had a fireplace used for heat and cooking, and to the right was the stairway to the second level.

In order to ensure that her only brother would take care of *Nonno,* like she had, my mother signed over her house to my uncle and his wife. My mother could have made use of the money by selling the house, but it was needed as insurance for *Nonno's* care.

We travelled by car to the busy city of Napoli where we were to board the ocean liner *Homeland.* With the eyes and ears of a five-year-old child, I witnessed my mother and older sister heartbroken, scared, tearful, and excited all at the same time.

I may not have fully understood it, but I knew and sensed that this was going to be a long and hard trip to overcome. To this day, I can still recall how scared and worried my mother was, being on the huge ship for so many days and nights, and hoping we would not encounter too many storms. *"Dio, ci protegga,"* she would often say, imploring God to protect us.

Many people she knew had made the same trip before us, and once they had settled in the new country they would write to their loved ones back home about their experiences; some good, some with regret and disappointment at the hardships they encountered: disillusionment with job prospects; frustration with language and cultural barriers; marriages by proxy that went awry; and alcoholism and domestic violence, to name a few. The stories from those letters were heard all over the neighbourhood.

But now the time had come for us to embark upon our journey. *"Vogghiu mu vaju alla casa, mamma,"* I cried as we walked up to board the ship.

My sister Virginia tried to comfort me. *"Andiamo a casa, Franca,"* she replied. "We are going home."

But in my mind, I wanted to go back to the home we had just left behind.

We were assigned a cabin on the main upper deck. "How lucky you are to be in a cabin, to be able to walk out into the fresh, cool air," I heard people saying to my mother.

Some of our fellow passengers had cabins in the lower sections of the ship. Sometimes you could see fish swim by the little porthole windows, which made you feel very uncomfortable to think how far under water you were sleeping.

The first two days were peaceful and uneventful, but as the *Homeland* travelled into deeper waters of the Atlantic Ocean they became rough, dark, and stormy. Other than leaving to go to the dining room for meals, we were confined to our cabin. The dining room was down a few floors from us. My brother and I would eat our food and were happy to see a lot of other people and kids just like us.

The food on the boat was very good and I was astonished at how lovely the tables were, set with white tablecloths and white dishes, and how courteous and attentive the waiters were to us.

Being young children, we had never experienced this kind of attention before.

A few days later, my mother and older sister Sara were seasick and I remember telling my mother that my brother and I wanted to eat. My mother was not sure she could send us with twelve-year old Virginia to the dining room alone. Virginia wanted to eat too, so we went. She knew the way down, and she knew our table. My mother was not only seasick, but worried until we got back.

A beautiful young lady was also sharing the cabin with us. She did not seem happy to be there. On the second day at sea, she started to get seasick. The next day she was violently sick and from her cot, she yelled, *"Managgia Cristoforo Colombo che ha scoperto l'America, ed i genitori che mi hanno mandato per sposarmi."* She cursed Christopher Columbus for having discovered America, and her parents for sending her to Canada to be married to someone she had never met. She was like a passport, making the way for other members of her family to follow in her footsteps.

My mother arranged for a little soup and lemon water to be brought to her and tried to give her some encouragement. *"Coraggio, signorina. Ti devi fare forte.* You have to stay strong."

August 3rd, 1953. We landed in Halifax, Canada at Pier 21. After twelve long days and nights on the sometimes stormy waters of the Atlantic Ocean, we were back on dry land and in our new country. Arriving at Pier 21 was very scary because no one spoke Italian and most of us spoke no English. We all filed down the boardwalk, each family trying to keep their children together. My mother did the same. "Sara, you take Bruno's hand. And Virginia, you take Franca's hand." Mother carried the two suitcases. The big trunk would follow later. Mother had loaded it with linens, towels, sheets, bedspreads, and some of her pots and pans.

As we entered a huge building, we were very well received. I know now that the people helping us immigrants were officers of the Salvation Army. They were dressed in black and the ladies wore little black hats tied under their chin. They gave us milk, cookies, and something we had never seen before, a 'sandwich' of white, sliced bread. We unwrapped it, looked at it, and took a bite. And out of our mouths it came. The bread stuck to the roof of our mouth. Little did we know that we would learn to love it.

After a few hours, we were to board a train to Montreal; and from there, another train to a small station in Emsdale, Ontario. We climbed on board the train but, alas, it was very heart-rending. The train was fuelled by coal and there was black coal soot everywhere, the seats, windows, and floor. Mother tried to keep Bruno and I still so we would go to sleep, but we wanted to play. Together on those seats and floor, we got ourselves pitch black, which presented another challenge for mother to clean us up. Finally, exhaustion set upon us and we slept.

Some hours later, we woke up to mother gently calling our names. We had arrived at the small station in Emsdale. This is where my uncle and his family had come before us, and where father was waiting for his family. Emsdale was approximately five miles from our new home, Kearney, Ontario. My mother was thankful to have the family all safe at the end of our voyage.

With tears, hugs, and prayers, we all stepped off the train and walked towards Father and our new life. The two older girls, Sara and Virginia, even if they did not completely remember our father's face, at least knew more about him. My brother Bruno, and me, the two youngest, hardly remembered him. But seeing our mother run towards him, and then hug and kiss him, we knew that this was *lu patri*, our father.

We hung back, a little anxious. We called out, "*Mamma! Mamma!*" But Father came towards us, picked us up with love in his eyes and kisses for all of us. He took us by our hands and led us to the waiting car.

Our uncle welcomed us and drove us to our new home in Kearney. By the time we got there, it was dark. We entered a huge building. Our apartment was upstairs on the second floor. A long hallway led us to two bedrooms. We all went to bed tired.

The next morning we took a look around. There was a big, white house right next door that belonged to Mr. Shaw. He was the owner of the building that we lived in. Downstairs, he had a grocery store where most of the people of the town did their day-to-day shopping. Most fruits and vegetables were not available there, but in the fall, you could buy apples. You couldn't buy fresh meat, either, just frozen.

I think Mother got the shock of her life. She had imagined that things would be hard, but all we had were the beds, kitchen table and chairs, a wood stove, and an outhouse. And no running water. The wood stove had to be lit every morning. To the side of the stove was a little tank you filled with water, and as you used the stove for heat and cooking, the water would warm up. You had to get the water outside at the well, by using the hand pump. Then you had to carry the full galvanized pails upstairs to use as needed.

In the winter, you always made sure to have extra water or you would have to melt snow, because sometimes the pump handle would freeze. You needed warm water to get the pump working again.

Sara was usually the one to take Bruno and me to the outhouse at the end of the yard during the day. We used a white enamel potty for the night. In Italy we had a bathroom inside the house, but it did not flush. We kept a pail of water next to it and used the pail of water as needed.

My father had prepared the kitchen with a few dishes and glasses, but it was a good thing that Mother had thought to bring a few pots and pans with her.

We lived on the main road in the village. There were a few other stores, a hotel, and a post office up the street. Across the road there was what looked like to me a huge lake. It was peaceful and calm. Over on the other side, you could see a house here and there.

Bruno and I did not start school that September. We were still too young. Virginia attended. The school was quite a walk from home. It was a one-room schoolhouse, grades one to eight, each grade in a row next to each other. It was kept warm in winter by a wood stove. The older boys would split and carry in the wood. It was always toasty warm.

I always wondered how Virginia managed in the beginning. She knew her mathematics very well, sometimes even surprising the teacher, but how did she begin to understand what the teacher was saying in the English language? The language barrier must have been hard to overcome. Virginia was a rock in our life. She was the one to go to the store and anywhere else when the need arose.

As the winter of '53 began to set in, the days got shorter and life became a little harder. Father did not own a car so both he and Virginia had to walk to work and school every day. The school was about a mile from our home, and the factory was even further. And we had never experienced winter with so much snow before. We had never needed boots or heavy coats.

In Italy we had only seen snow a couple of times at most in the winter months, but there had been so little of it, that by noon it would have all melted. This was a time when all the children would have fun picking up the snow and throwing it at each other.

Virginia now needed a good heavy coat, hat, and boots. She and Father were the only ones going out every day. These items and anything else we needed were ordered from Simpson Sears and the Eaton's catalogue. You would order the items you needed according to your age and size. It would take about eight to ten days for the parcel to arrive by mail. Then you went to the post office and picked it up. If the items did not fit, or weren't suitable, you just returned the parcel to the post office, and it would be shipped back, without a fee.

That first winter was very hard for Mother and Sara especially. They had no place to go. It wasn't like back home in Serra San Bruno, where they could visit family and friends and go to the grocery store, with no language barrier. And where she would take us to *l'asilo*, a daycare where we would be looked after by nuns, while mother went to work for a few hours in the garden of a local landowner.

Mother and Sara couldn't speak to anyone other than family, so every afternoon they would sit in front of the kitchen window facing the street overlooking the lake, and cry their eyes out over what they had left behind in Italy. I often heard my mother wondering if she had made the right choice by coming to Canada. The love of her husband and love for her children is what made up for everything and kept her going on.

Bruno and I were young, so we just took our surroundings and new life in stride. We were fed and kept clean and we didn't have to do any work. On the other hand, Mother and Sara had to get the wood stove lit in the morning, make sure there was enough water from the pump outside, carry in the wood from the cords piled up outside on the side of the house, and do the laundry for six people by hand.

There were a few other people in Kearney who spoke some Italian. Mr. Bonazza would come over often to talk to Mother and Sara. He would encourage them and speak of spring. The cold and snow would disappear and the sun would bring the warmer weather they craved. He told us about his huge garden and how much he enjoyed working in it. He had two older sons and a daughter. Two were married and had families of their own. As time went on, we met these people, and life did not seem so isolated and lonely.

Sometimes on Sunday, our uncle from Emsdale would come to our house with his family and stay for a meal with us. These were the best days for us. He would bring over his record player and play some Italian music. This made everyone happy and his two younger daughters would even dance together.

That first Christmas in Canada was very different. In Italy, we didn't have Santa Claus. The *befana*, or Christmas witch, arrived on January 6th, the Epiphany, leaving us a little bag with a tangerine, a few chocolate coins, some walnuts, and maybe a pair of socks. She never left us a piece of coal, the traditional gift for naughty children.

On Christmas morning in Canada, we got a surprise. Mr. Shaw came over with gifts for everyone and toys for Bruno and me. We were happy to see so much. There was a doll and playhouse for me, and a truck and little cars for Bruno. We even got a sled. The older girls got hats, gloves, and a scarf each. Mother and Father offered Mr. Shaw coffee and *biscotti* that she had made. Mr. Shaw had shown us how generous and good people could be to newcomers.

The cold days and nights were long. We had no television but we did have a radio. Every night from about six to eight we enjoyed listening to popular country music by Johnny Cash, Patsy Cline, Buddy Holly, Doris Day, and other singers. Bruno and I even learned to sing along to some parts of *"Peggy Sue"* by Buddy Holly and *"You Belong To Me,"* by Patsy Cline, among others.

It must have been very hard for my father and mother, with very little money and no knowledge of the English language or the ways of a new country. But slowly we started to get used to life here. Although in some ways it was harder than in Italy, we were all together. We knew we were here to stay. With the coming of spring and plans to start a garden like Mr. Bonazza, the family went on each and every day with the hope of better times coming our way.

In the next four years, three more siblings were born: Joanne, Nicky, and Rita. We were seven children in all. Father was still working at the coal factory, but he came to the realization that he needed to consider a move to a larger city to ensure a better future for us all. Sara and Virginia were young ladies now, and they needed opportunities to meet other people and find employment.

We had relatives in Sudbury, in the Gatchell neighbourhood to be exact. Father's sister Assunta and her family lived here. She told Father to come to Sudbury and stay with them. They already owned their own home.

Father came to Sudbury alone. He found a job right away, working on the construction of the Federal Building on Lisgar Street. The next step was to bring Virginia. By this time Virginia had the English language conquered and even Bruno and I had been going to school for three years, so we understood and spoke English well.

Virginia found a job at a dry cleaners when she was sixteen and then she and Father had to find an apartment in order to be able to bring the rest of the family to Sudbury. But this was not an easy task. Sudbury was beginning to grow as a city, mostly with people like us immigrants who also had relatives help them come over and start a new life. Apartments were not easy to rent or find, especially for a family of nine. Homeowners would rather rent their apartments to smaller families or young couples.

About a month after starting the search, Father and Virginia found someone who rented us a one-storey, two-bedroom house in Minnow Lake. It had a basement—something I had never seen— and a backyard with a few trees and a big black rock slab from which we would survey the houses below.

I remember being excited about moving from Kearney. We knew we had aunts, uncles, and cousins in Sudbury. We had heard from Father and Virginia that it was a much bigger town with lots of Italian people and families just like us.

School in Minnow Lake was very different from Kearney. Here the school was down the street from our house. I was in grade three and there was a full classroom of boys and girls. This was a much more advanced school than the one-room schoolhouse in Kearney. Just to see all the children lining up each morning, class by class, before we entered the school, was new to me and Bruno.

Mother also had an easier life here. The stove was not wood-burning; it was electric. You just turned on a knob. The water for cooking and laundry came from a faucet, hot or cold. We also had a toilet you could flush and a bathtub.

Once a week, Father and Mother would go to downtown Sudbury to do the weekly groceries at an Italian store called B & P, right at the end of Durham Street. You were able to buy anything you needed there. Best of all, they would deliver your groceries later that same day. Few families around our neighbourhood had cars; like our parents, they took the city bus to go downtown, which was a bustling centre at that time.

Sara was able to find a job. She was very happy to be able to go to work at Cecutti's Bakery, which at that time, was located downtown. There, she met a young lady with whom she is still friends to this day. Sara would take the bus to and from work. Even that was a new experience.

We eventually moved to the Gatchell neighbourhood and as the years went by, each of us found a place in this new life in Sudbury. I went to work at a local grocery store called Gatchell Meat Market. I walked to work every day and would even go home at lunchtime, and then back to the store until closing time at six p.m. I enjoyed my job because most of my neighbours and friends shopped there. The owners were good people to work for and we all got to know each other very well.

Two years later I met a young Italian man named Pasquale Lisi.

I knew from the first moment I met him that I would marry him. Pat and I were married eighteen months later.

When I stand back and look at my sons Robert and David with their children—my five grandchildren—I am proud to be Italian and equally proud and thankful to be a Canadian. The courage, hardships and struggles of my parents and the lessons we learned as children, made us who we are today.

On Being Franco-Ontarian
By Julie-Anne Bolduc

"I'm from Northern Ontario," I say because it's easier.

"Oh, you mean Barrie or Sudbury?"

You know there's a whole other half of Ontario past those two cities, right?

This is what I want to say, but my mom raised me to be polite.

"I grew up in a small city near Thunder Bay, in the Longlac and Hearst area," I respond.

Usually I can see their eyes bulge out as their brains explode. Cannot compute.

"There are places further north?"

I can understand their confusion. I grew up surrounded by a culture they know nothing about.

The drive north is always a pleasant one. The trees surround you like a protective sanctuary. I always feel at peace whenever I go home, near nature. A few of my family members still come back every summer, seeking the solitude and quietness only the north can provide.

I love going home. It's not just nature but the language. I want to dive right into the mix of French and English. Yet, I'm always a little nervous whenever I go home. I overthink my French and confuse my words. Living in-between languages can be difficult at times. I guess it's like putting on an old dress. The old dress doesn't always fit right because you've gained twenty pounds or you've lost some. Sometimes I forget words or mispronounce them. Often, I feel guilty because after having spoken French my whole life, I should be able to speak it better. It's not that I don't want to surround myself with the French language. The pull of the English language is like a magnet seducing me with its constant presence. Yet inside I yearn for my own language and heritage.

During the summer, I look forward to seeing everyone in Longlac; those family members that can make it to camp for as long as work permits them. We fish, laugh, share stories, swim, take saunas, build fires and fish some more.

Going home offers a piece of serenity I can hold onto. It's my family, heritage and roots, all in one little geographic area. It calls me – capable of replenishing me spiritually, psychologically and emotionally. We gather at my uncle's place every year. It's a second home where we can reconnect with family and those scattered across Canada.

I get to see my "favourite Uncle from the South" who has driven twenty hours to get there. As we all sit around waiting for the annual fish fry, I slide my lawn chair closer to my uncle, grinning, showing him all my teeth. I can't help but feel like a little girl. No matter how old I get, I can always see my ten-year-old self reflected back at me in his eyes.

"Can you tell me, *Mon Oncle*?" I ask.

"Tell you what?"

I love sitting beside him and listening to his stories. He has a quiet manner about him. I can see some grey starting to show through, but he'll always be a young uncle to me. I think it's part of

150 YEARS UP NORTH AND MORE

his charm. He's a child at heart.

Like most Catholic families, my mom comes from a very large family. My *Mémère* had nine kids. I have a tough time imagining giving birth to one, let alone nine. I always joke that I want my future child teleported out of me.

"Well, can you tell me about when you were younger and what it was like? You started yesterday, but then you took your grand-kids fishing. I want to hear it all," I say with a bigger smile, hoping to coax it out of him.

He chuckles. I can just imagine his brain searching among all those memories. He tells me how he used to go out hunting by himself behind his house until an old man saw a wolf trailing not far behind him. That put an end to his solo hunting trips.

"I love our history," I tell him. "I love learning about our culture. It's rich and so different. I always find it difficult when people from other areas of Ontario, Canada or even the world, correct us or criticize our different dialect."

We should be proud of our slang and differences, since that's what makes us special. We speak French and English interchange-ably, making our own language. Frenglish is a language with its own set of rules. I try to explain it to my Anglophone friends, but I can't.

"Remember the *Bonhomme Sept-Heure?*" he asks.

"Yes! Was he like the boogeyman?"

"He was much scarier than some boogeyman," my uncle responds. "I think in English he'd be called the Bonesetter. Our parents would use him as a threat like the boogeyman. He was like a chiropractor or a doctor who would come at seven o'clock to 'fix' you. All he did was hurt you."

"AYOYE!!"

"We'd have to be in bed before seven o'clock, and when it turned seven we could hear our parents complaining and yelling how he was hurting them."

30

"Well, you know, I'm very glad that's not a tradition my mom continued."

He smiles. "Well, let's see, what else?"

I drag my chair closer. He points to my cup and chuckles.

"You know, when we used to go to my Uncle's place in Hearst, we all shared the same cup? Boiled water from what we called *une bomb* (boiler) over *poele* (oven). It was a special cup."

"You're kidding," I laugh.

"Nope. We all used it and put it back. We could be twenty people using the same cup. Now, I really doubt people would be okay with all of us sharing."

I hold my cup closer, happy to not share it with the thirty people sitting around us; surprised at how much life has changed in such a short span of time.

He tells me I'm lucky that we have toilets now. Back then they would have had to use what they called the Catherine. This was kept inside and used only by women. It was basically a pot with a cover over top of it. The men went outside or used the *bécosse*. The men would use the *bécosse* or pee behind the barn, even when it was -40 outside.

"You know," he continues ignoring my disgusted look, "we didn't have electricity dere till the '50s."

I'm appalled. "The '50s!!!"

"Yup."

He says, 'dere', the same as most northerners do, with an accent that tends to get thicker the longer we are together.

Like each culture, we have our own slang and sayings, but we still can't help but tease each other. My uncle tells me about a friend who's very French and had gone to visit them. He said she told them a "black nun was coming." His wife looked outside, worried she meant something ominous. She meant to say it was getting dark outside. The word is spelled *noirceur* but sounds like *noire-soeur*.

I laughed so hard I snorted water out of my nose. Translations aren't always quite so direct. We joke about closing the lights when we really mean to turn them off. Or we want to pass the broom or put the volume down when we want to sweep the floor or lower the volume.

"*Touer – tu trouveras ça froid!* What temperatures we have now aren't comparable," he says.

Toi pronounced *touer*, might sound odd to other French speakers, but we all embrace it like a warm hot chocolate on a frosty day. In Northern Ontario we like to add the little extra "er" at the end of *toi* (you).

As we all sit around eating fish, my nephew, who has spoken mostly French his whole life, talks about how he made that mistake once. He was trying to say, *"J'ai chaud pour toi"*, which would mean you look so warm with all those layers, even I can feel the heat. Yet my nephew went for the literal translation and accidentally told his friend, "I'm so hot for you".

Another family favourite to say in English is: "Your mother, your shovel." This is a direct translation from French and a bit of a play on words and idioms. This is a perfect example of a Frenglish joke. What we're implying and trying to say is: *ta mère, t'appelle*, which means, "your mother is calling you or would like to see you." The word *t'appelle* sounds like *ta pelle* which means shovel. Thus, we get "your mother, your shovel."

We all love our reunions. More than just time spent together, it's tradition and a time to share stories. Whenever I hear about these times, I can't help but feel somewhat envious or sad that we have lost this sense of community. Now it seems the only way to see each other is through our digital worlds. Luckily, we do have these to keep us together somehow.

My mom likes to tell me about the *réveillons* they used to have

32

every year when everyone lived in Longlac for Christmas. It was a very huge affair. My mom says she would put us to bed and then wake us up after mass because everyone would come over around 1:00 a.m. for a huge supper. I used to love singing the *chansons à répondre* (answering songs).

"What kind of songs did you guys sing, Mom?"

"Oh wow, it's been ages. Let's see. Oh!! There's *V'la le bon vent* and *Au Champ de l'Alouette*. She starts singing, *"Au chant de l'alouette, je veille et je dors. J'écoute à l'alouette et puis je m'en dors."*

I join in singing the last line. "I remember that one mom!" I exclaim. "I remember singing that one a lot."

"I thought you might. It's more of a children's song. You know, I always miss your *Mémère* during these times. We used to *faire la popottes* during the holidays. We would bake forty *tourtières* and split them between each other."

Popotte doesn't translate as well, but usually means to cook or bake together. *Tourtières* are known as French-Canadian meat pies.

For a *tourtière*, we would usually use beef with onions and sometimes potatoes, depending on how adventurous we would get. Some of us would add ketchup to the mix. It's still one of my favourite dishes.

"I know we tried to make some last year, Mom, and all we did was manage to make twenty split between all of us. I can't imagine making that many *tourtières*." I continue, "But mom, we still do all that in a way. We all get together, but we don't play those old school games of yours though."

"Do you remember those nights, when you were younger?"

"I remember being exhausted and falling asleep in church."

"You were so cute in your little outfits. My poor little kids, half asleep and grumpy," she laughs and continues. "Well, it was a little different because we'd come back after and have an even bigger meal than the last one. It was called the *réveillons* for a reason. We stayed up all night and went to bed in the morning at three or even four o'clock. We'd wake up for lunch and all head to *Mémère's* for lunch and have *la soup à Mémère.*

"Well, now we're lucky if everyone stays up past two o'clock." I add. "I remember you saying that after the second supper we would open the gifts from aunts, uncles and parents."

"Yes, and then we would send you guys back to bed to wait pour *le Père Noel.* He only came once you were asleep to fill your stockings and put gifts under the tree."

Every year we all listen with a smile as she talks about the big reunions we had as kids. This is still somewhat how we celebrate our Christmas. It's a massive affair and we always try to focus on the togetherness of it all. We still give some gifts, but my favourite part is having everyone sleeping in one house for three to four days, driving each other crazy with games, drinks, outside activities, great food, and gifts.

My mom puts her wine glass in the air, starts pretending she's incredibly drunk and sings, *"ont boiras pas toujours de l'eau, nous ne sommes pas des grenouilles,"* which means, "we aren't frogs, so we won't always be drinking water," or something like that. Eventually, I learnt through my uncle that it was something my pépère used to say.

"We would all gather on a regular evening together and take out the instruments and just play. There wasn't really a special reason or occasion," my uncle says, drawing me out of my reverie.

"We used to visit my *Pépère* in Hearst for Christmas day, but back then we didn't have clear roads everywhere and most weren't paved. He picked us up *au grand chemin* (highway) early in the morning because we couldn't get to his place by car. When he picked us up in Hearst, he drove a *borleau* (sleigh) with his sssshfal. The kids would sit in the seat at the front and the adults would stand in the back in the box. *Pépère* always had a cow pelt that he would use to keep himself warm and then throw over us when he picked us up. We would eat *râgout de pates de cochon avec des biscuits à la molasse et une tarte aux raisins avec d'la soupe et du pain frais.*" His descriptions sound wonderful to me. Delicious homemade meals from his youth, passed down from each generation.

"Then we would all listen to la Bolduc, play games and someone would tell stories," he says.

Sometimes my uncle would play the violin and *Mémère* and her sister, *tante* Juliette, would play the accordion. I remember going to visit *Mémère* and that's what she played for us - La Bolduc. I still have her song, *j'ai un boutton sur le bout de la langue*, stuck in my head. I still listen to it when I miss her.

This wonderful piece of my past sings through my veins with each lyric. In my rough singing voice I start singing the few words that I can remember from La Bolduc'and my favourite song by her. *"Pis j'en ai un su' l' bout d' la langue, qui m'empêche de turluter."*

My uncle and I laugh. Clearly, I'm not a talented singer. La Bolduc is a famous French-Canadian singer from the 1930s. She was known as the Queen of Canadian folk singing. While we weren't related, she was still an important part of my youth and heritage.

We all share a fading culture and language. Slowly every generation speaks more and more English. The loss of my *Mémère* reminds me of the loss of traditions and my heritage, which I do my best to hold on to.

Some might call this assimilation and others, annihilation. But I hope for a resurgence. I am proud to be Franco-Ontarian.

Her Woven Memory
By Kim Fahner

I) Of Visitation(s) and Imagination(s)...

In her mind, in her memory, there was a long road, stretching down a craggy western shore. It made its way to Cobh, snaking southwards along hillsides and shorelines where rock tumbles too sharply into ocean without warning. When she walked down a stretch of that road some time ago, a long line of people rose up in her mind, bent under the weight of loss, death, grief, and eviction; following that road, dragging their feet down that western shore. On their way, they must have heard tell of how the ships in Queenstown sometimes left packed, so full of people, and then arrived in Boston, New York, or Montreal so many weeks later, nearly empty. Coffin or famine ships they called them, knowing people were frail and unhealthy as they boarded, and then checked off as names lost on a roster as they crossed the sea, consecrated to the waves and raised up only in memory. Her people had walked this way, then, a century and a half before her, leaving lives and family behind, all in hopes that Canada would be the place to root, again, anew.

In her mind, which was rooted twentieth century Canadian by all rights, measures, and origins of birth, she could vividly imagine the sea crossing if she wanted to. She thought of Michael and Darby Kelly, and of how they came to settle in the Ottawa Valley. It began, this imagining, with the sound of waves crashing on the shores of a Great Lake. She could lay herself out in the depths of a humid August night, star-fished in a short blue silk nightgown, on the hard mattress of a borrowed summer bed, in a rented cottage on the edge of Lake Erie, and listen to the sound of that Great Lake's waves with her eyes closed. That pulsing coursed through her, water shaking land, like the heartbeat of a longed-for lover. On the rainiest of days she would sit at that upper window, sash thrown open, nose pressed to the screen like a little girl day-dreaming, looking out over bird houses and big trees, watching Erie breathe itself into being. It conjured itself with magic. She knew that, even if others didn't.

With the sound of big waves in her ears, she imagined how that ship—the one that had carried her people across the sea—would have looked: tall and stately, but battered and worn. It would, she thought, not be too much unlike herself. It might have had grand sails once, wide wood planks to walk across—with or without sea legs—and a sheen of brine glazed across its masts in dawn's light. It might have carried thousands, back and forth across the Atlantic, baptized in salt water and blessed by a withered priest. It might have crossed rough waters and passages, back and forth, for years before it had brought her ancestors here to Canada, after the Famine, with all of them starving in body and so defeated in spirit. It would be, despite its lengthy journeys, strong and solid and true, this imagined ship.

These maternal ancestors arrived in Canada, then. Some of them. Some were left behind, in Waterford, or Ennis, or Limerick, or Clare. Where they came from really didn't matter, when all was

150 YEARS UP NORTH AND MORE

said and done. They were lost, and then found, evicted, and then resettled. From a place where potatoes once grew happily, in fields that sloped down to the fierce sea, where greens came in shades that weren't easily categorized in Pantone colours, they cast off, not wanting to leave, but knowing that this place in the Ottawa Valley—so far away now—was a place that took in the Irish. They had been rooted in a village called Clough, a Gaelic name that sounds like 'clock' when you say it out loud, but they lost themselves, and their place of birth origin, because of the potato blight. They had walked those roads and fields for centuries, somehow married into a spare Scottish family from Barra in the Outer Hebrides, melded, made more Celts, and never imagined having to leave it, that place where the veil is thin between worlds. This is the place where the seen and the unseen dance together, weaving and unweaving themselves into spirals. But some of these descended women carried the dance with them, across the sea, and walk still with its heavy gifts of sight and foresight, more than a century and a half onwards now.

Maternal. From the Latin, *mater*, for mother. From her side, Irish, all of this comes: this ancestry, this storied past. From her side, then, with names like Kelly, and Ennis, Delaney, and Power, come the gifts of knowing, and not knowing, and then becoming comfortable with intuition, and seeing, and hearing, and sensing. From her mother's side, then, all things mystical and magical. Maternal. From the side that her own mother did not believe in, closed up and pulled in, afraid of things she couldn't explain even until the day she died, when she saw the shade of her father at the end of her hospital bed. Now, this daughter made by mother, this one, searches, all quest and journey, outward but mostly inwards, finding star systems inside skin, at core of heart, where a galaxy now spins within a rib cage.

And so, they came, with sea salt in their hair, all too pale skin and clear crystalline eyes, knowing more of sorrow than of joy, even if they kept it close and didn't speak of it out loud. And then, they moved northwards, towards the nickel and copper veins that ran deep under the earth, hidden. One man, her great-grandfather, was a purveyor of goods, a merchant for immigrant miners. In Creighton he owned a general store, managed the post office, dressed his girls in the finest clothing and his sons in the very best of well turned out and tailored suits. He was a Kelly, named James Cornelius. His wife, Alice, was a Delaney by birth, and her people were by way of Pembroke. Later, in the late 1940s, it was he who built a big white house with shutters that were painted green, on Kingsmount, the place of kings, the hill where you could see the far black rocks where the men dumped slag, the Gatchell sky alight at night with flames, timed so that you could set your watch by it.

One of James and Alice's girls, also named Alice, would marry an Ennis, a man called Len, a man who came from Pembroke, too, and who managed a mine. Those two, a fine pair at first, had five children, three boys and two girls. Later, they would part, no longer finding kindness or love in one another, their hearts drifting. These are the trees that people do not wish to speak of, the ones full of gnarled branches, hidden secrets, shameful stories. You can draw your tree, she thinks one night, while she walks along a Pelee Island beach gathering stones and sea glass in her pockets, but you cannot know all there is to know of the past. You were not a part of that, she tells herself, so all can now be imagined, created, gathered up and retold as only the best fiction can be. So, she does. She writes a story about an Irish Catholic family, renames it, creates new children and erases others, plants herself on the outside, looking in, imagining how love arrives, flourishes, and then erases itself (without guilt or conscience) so that people pretend it never existed. That stymies her, she knows, how a love or a life story is so easily manipulated and shaded in new colours, depending on who tells it, or who hears it, or who lives it, or who rewrites it in new ways. And sooner, rather than later, the stories are more fiction than fact, but echoes of truth ring through them, rippling along through the centuries, from a place of lack to one of possibility.

II) and of final farewells...

Some days are darker than others. This last Kelly, Clare, one of ten, died in her mid-90s, curled up on a nursing home bed, her mind lost, caught up in imagined and cinematic memories of her youth: of gingham day dresses and black Oxfords; of long Catholic Masses said in Latin and bathed in incense—all holy candles flickering in shadow, all rosaries clicking in wooden pews; of picnics on Lake Ramsey when trees were still sparse and rocks were black as pitch; of family dinners with twelve seated around a night table, passing potatoes, new carrots, and roasts bathed in homemade gravy on fine Limoges china; of a man who courted her, falsely, even though he was married, offering her bits of jewelry and perfume; of the men who longed for her deeply, when she was a beauty, in the 1930s and 40s, but who never could imagine living with the threat of a wild Irish wife; of fine whiskey drunk from crystal tumblers on Patrick's holiest of days—proof of having come up from beneath, from having risen from a poverty that came with them from across the sea—and of songs sung under a dining room table, a face flushed and full of life; and of those nieces and nephews who loved her, even those called 'grand', who played games of hide and seek with her in the big back Sudbury garden, all wide green leaves, all peonies and poppies and lilacs.

And then, this one: this grand-niece who thinks of how that one woman was the last original one whom she had known and loved, this old woman who was one of ten children, who was named after County Clare, spelled without the "i" throughout her life, her parents embodying their family history in her naming and

40

christening. And of a late July day in a Northern graveyard, and a bottle of Tullamore Dew tipped upside down into a grave, then splashed against a stone, and a few words of thanks to those who came before, all generations lined up and gathered round that head stone, ghosts and shades of those who crossed the sea, who survived the Great Hunger, and even a prayer said in heart's passing for those who came far, far before them.

Lately, she thinks, doors close behind her, decades and centuries disappear, become branches on a family tree, so that she can now move forward, opening new doors and pulling up old sashed windows in a heart that might have once painted them over for good measure and solely out of fear. Lately, she thinks, these open windows and doors are best, so that birds escape from imagined cage of ribs, wings wide and feathered, no longer fearful, flying out and into this heart's new sky.

III) and of Recreation(s) of Self…

Now, she adorns herself with silvered spirals, these triskeles: tiny Celtic symbols from Newgrange that speak of prehistoric trinities, of earth, sky, and sea. She roots herself in Nature and the wildest of landscapes. There will be no trinity of motherhood for her, no mention of that one's maid, mother, and crone. She is in a middle place, between worlds, fashioning her own spaces and leaving them unnamed, preferring to touch the bark of tall trees, reaching up to stroke leaves in passing, speaking softly to them as they listen, bending down to her, waiting for her to sing songs of tales yet to be told.

In this middle place, she thinks, she will wander, from here to there (but maybe not back again), from north to south, east to west, curling herself into spirals now, not wanting to be boxed in, named, or pinned to a cork board like a stolen monarch or swallowtail with pierced wings. In this middle place, at the centre of that triskele, at the core of the thing itself, in a place of origin, she will dance a ceili, twirl in a whirl, challenge those who wish to define and confine her.

She will refuse, in this middle place, in this ancient and sacred space between worlds, where the veil is thin as a spider's web, to be caught or trapped. She will drape herself in gossamer, walk down to Erie's shore in twilight, wait for the wind to kiss her lips. Then, she will drop that cape, walk out into the bluest of waters. Then, she will feel the strong push and pull, allow its waves to move her, transport and transform her, baptize her in ancient and druidic ways.

And when she emerges, newly born, like a nymph from water, like a dragonfly with new wings, she will take up her gossamer train again, walk amidst the grove of sacred trees, palms pressed intimate to their trunks, and listen now to their songs. In this middle place, in these years, she will blossom and bloom, triumphant and operatic, voice no longer silenced, heart no longer trapped, but with wings wide and expectant.

My Story
By Hussein Qarqouz *

*As told to Laura Stradiotto

I'm from Al-Qusayr, Syria, a city about thirty-five kilometres south of Homs. Syria is a beautiful country, but in 2011 we started having problems and many people started demonstrating in the streets for a new President. Fifty years with the same family in power. Police killed people every day.

One day I went to go open my bakery and police questioned me about being in the demonstration. They took me to jail. I was tortured from morning until night for two and a half months.

I was in a small room with about fifty to sixty people and I wasn't sure if I would live or die. One night I spoke to my friend in jail and in the next morning he was gone. I was scared for my family. I didn't know how they were doing or what they were doing for food.

Thank God, my family is here with me today. But my oldest brother died in jail in Syria, my youngest brother is still in jail in Syria.

Before the war, I worked in Lebanon for ten years while my

family lived in Syria.

My first son, Mohammad, was born in 2003 when I was working in Lebanon. I would visit my family every three months for a few days. When Ousama was born in 2005 I asked myself, "why do I work in Lebanon when my family is in Syria?" I decided to move back to Syria to open a bakery and restaurant.

I built a big, beautiful house. Everything was new. I loved my house. I worked ten years just to build that house, but within one hour of bombing there was nothing.

Life became hard. Bombs. Bombs. Bombs. The army surrounded my house. I was scared they would kill my family.

There was no hospital and there were no doctors. Everyone moved away because it wasn't safe. Lots of people needed to eat. So, I would open my restaurant at six o'clock in the morning and close at six o'clock in the night. And I fed them for free.

It only got worse. Every day people died.

One day I woke up at four o'clock in the morning and it was quiet. Two minutes later, a bomb fell about four metres from me. The next day, five airplanes dropped bombs in my city. I took my son by the hand and ran down the street. I decided, no more. I needed to move.

My friend helped my family escape to Lebanon by car and then for six hours we walked in the bush. We left at two o'clock in the morning so the police wouldn't see us. If we were caught, they would have shot us.

We lived in a refugee camp in Lebanon for three and a half years, but there was no future for my boys. My son Nabil was nine years old and had never been to school.

I worked for the city as a gardener, but it wasn't safe so I decided to visit the United Nations Embassy. I had lots of friends who worked in Canada and I kept hearing that it was a good country.

People are very good here, helping refugees with a big smile. You have a good Prime Minister. I think Canada is the best country.

And the boys look Canadian with their red hair.

In Canada, everything was new. I didn't know the language. The loneliness was the most difficult. I missed my brothers, my sisters, my cousins, my community.

People told me to keep going. The St. Andrew's group was very good to us, even driving my wife to English lessons. Our first winter in Canada was very cold. The second winter was better and now, it's no problem.

After two weeks in Canada, I realized I needed a job. I still had family in Syria that needed to eat too. In Lebanon, I have two sisters and two brothers. In Syria, near the border of Turkey, I have two brothers and one sister. There is nothing for them there. No work, no money, no food.

One month after I arrived, I started working at Golden Grain Bakery. I worked with them for about one year, but after Christmas business was slow and I didn't have full-time work. I moved to Regency Bakery because they gave me full-time hours, but about six months later my father became sick with Alzheimer's Disease. He would leave the house and police would have to look for him. I couldn't work when my father was sick so I stayed home with him. My father cannot be in a hospital because he must stay home with me.

I decided I must open a bakery. Not in Toronto or Ottawa, but in Sudbury. In Canada, you have many vegetarian people, which is good for me. Half my menu is for just vegetarians: spinach, potatoes, falafels, vegetable soup, tabbouleh salad but also shawarmas, kebabs and sweets. It will be a family business called Damascus Coffee and Bakery.

Adrift
By Liisa Kovala

Life was drifting toward a new kind of normal for Aarne Kovala six years after the end of World War II. The sea still drew him to her, as he coasted from ship to ship in his home country of Finland and neighbouring Sweden. During the day he'd dream of the faraway shores of Australia as he meticulously painted and repaired the windjammers *Pommern* and *Passat*, but when it seemed the ships would not sail he abandoned them for work on a Swedish oil tanker, ready to embark on a sea voyage wherever the winds blew him.

Despite the freedom he relished during the day, at night Aarne was haunted by the memories of the war. The incessant barking of guard dogs, the cold steel of barbed wire fences, and the pungent odour of burning human flesh filled his dreams. The clipped heels of jackboots accompanied the faces of Nazi soldiers alongside those of his former shipmates, emaciated and sick from hunger and disease. Images of a restless sea were accompanied by the whirr of bombers, views of potato fields were shattered by the strafing of low-flying aircraft. Sights and sounds that kept sleep at bay, returning night after night when exhaustion finally claimed him.

Reclaiming his independence came in the form of work aboard the oil tanker, allowing him to sail between the ship's home port in Sweden and the exotic Caribbean Islands. Work gave Aarne purpose, and the ship allowed him to see the world.

On his rare days off, Aarne wandered around Stockholm, stopping to chat with people he knew. One afternoon, he noticed a familiar man signalling to him. It was an old friend with whom he'd worked aboard the oil tanker for many months. During the war, the sailor, an Estonian, rowed a small fishing boat through the night across the Baltic Sea to escape Russian occupied Estonia. He and his fellow escapees entered Sweden and found work in a bush camp where they struggled to learn Swedish.

"Aarne, I have some news," the sailor said. "Listen, I'm going to Canada. I'm going to pick up the application papers at the Canadian Embassy soon. Why don't you fill out the papers and come too?"

Aarne looked at him quizzically and considered it for a moment. "I guess it wouldn't hurt."

A few days later, Aarne's friend brought the papers to the ship, still docked in Stockholm's port. Aarne glanced at the questions, his pen hovering over the paper for several moments. In his tight cursive writing, he completed every section, stopping once in a while to ask his friend a question. "What now?" he asked when the forms were complete.

"I'll submit them tomorrow. It may be several weeks or even months before we get approval."

Aarne shrugged. "No problem. The ship is travelling to the Canary Islands in a few days, so we'll have to wait until we get back, I guess."

Some weeks later, the oil tanker was safely in Swedish waters again and Aarne was on shore leave. He remembered his application and wondered what had come of it.

150 YEARS UP NORTH AND MORE

Aarne walked to the steps of the Canadian Embassy in Stockholm. The Immigration Officer looked Aarne up and down. "Your application is approved, pending an X-Ray. In the meantime, go ahead and book a ticket for a passenger boat. If all goes well, you'll be on your way to Canada in no time."

Aarne clasped the officer's hand and smiled broadly, excited for a new adventure. As he left the Embassy, Aarne began to have second thoughts. Should he really sail across the world to a country he knew nothing about? Aarne brushed off his doubts and booked a passage out of Liverpool that left in a few weeks time.

Instead of returning to his job, Aarne gave his notice and decided to make a trip home to see his parents, Anna-Liisa and Jussi, and his older siblings, Heimo, Kalle, and Lyyli. This might be the last time he would see them for a very long time, he thought, as he prepared to tell them about his decision to leave.

Aarne remembered a similar encounter with his parents many years before. At fifteen, his brothers were fighting in the Winter War against the Russians, and World War II was raging. Too young to fight, he decided to leave his Baltic seaside town for the capital, Helsinki. Having lied about his age, he found work aboard the *S/S Wappu*, a merchant marine ship transporting war materials between Finland, Poland, and Germany. When the Finnish war with Russia ended, Finland's alliances with Germany were severed and the Finnish sailors, docked in the Polish port of Gdańsk, were arrested. At sixteen, Aarne became a prisoner in a Nazi concentration camp. He would not see his home again until after the war ended.

Now, Aarne confronted his family again about his life-changing decision.

"Oh, dear boy, how are you going to live there?" Anna-Liisa asked, concern written on her face as it had been all those years before. She knew she could do little to persuade her impetuous youngest child, who, at twenty-three, had become an independent, if unanchored young man. How could he leave the safety of his family now, after all he'd been through?

Wasn't he the son who'd hoarded food after every meal for months following his return home after the war? Wasn't he the young man who suffered from insomnia and woke to night terrors? After the trials he'd endured, Anna Liisa worried that he was making the wrong decision.

"I've heard they have bread there, too," Jussi said. Aarne had shared some details about his war experiences—the exhausting work, lack of food, and rampant diseases—enough for Jussi to know his son could survive anything.

Aarne said farewell to his family and his hometown, ready to embark on a new journey. From Oulu, he travelled through Sweden to Denmark, then on to England. When he arrived, immigration asked him for his visa.

"Visa?" Aarne asked. "I've been to England many times aboard ships and we were never asked for visas." Aarne stared at the immigration officer with bewilderment. "Listen, I'm on my way to Canada. I have my tickets and everything."

The officer shook his head, but stamped his papers. "Go on, now," he said, waving him through. Finally, Aarne boarded the ship for his passage to Quebec City and breathed a sigh of relief as he surveyed the vessel that would deliver him to a new world. Perhaps there he would feel less adrift than during his post-war years in Finland. Could he leave his horrific past behind by sailing away from the country of his youth?

On board the ship, Aarne relished the benefits of being a paid passenger, instead of an employee. He ate meals with the other passengers, strolled on deck, and partook of the leisure activities. While he wandered aimlessly around the boat, he happened to meet a young Norwegian man who was also a solo traveller.

"I'm on my way to Canada, too," the young man said. "Why don't we meet at the train station in Toronto? I'm going to be in Montreal for a few days, but then I'll travel by train to meet you."

Aarne knew nothing about Toronto, or the train station, or what day the Norwegian would arrive, but he agreed. In the meantime, after disembarking, he made his way from the port in Montreal to Toronto by train. There, he asked two ladies where he could find a room to rent. They directed him to a place on Wilcox Street.

A few days later, Aarne went to Union Station and searched the crowds for his new friend, wondering how many days he would need to come back before the Norwegian would appear. Aarne arrived at one o'clock, prepared to wait for a few hours, just in case, but to his surprise, through the hustle of the crowd, Aarne recognized the Norwegian making his way toward him.

"Welcome to Toronto. It's a good thing I came today. I wasn't sure if you'd be on this train," Aarne said. "I've found a room to rent already, so you are welcome to stay with me for now."

When they arrived at the house, Aarne approached the landlady. "Is it okay for my friend to stay here?"

The landlady agreed, and the Norwegian started unpacking. Before he was settled, Aarne overheard the landlady talking to some of her guests. "They're Finlanders, I think. I don't know what kind of bums they are. They haven't even paid their rent yet."

Aarne frowned. "Let's get out of here," he said to his friend. He paid the landlady for one week's rent, packed his suitcase, and the two left the boarding house for good. Before long they found a rental in the downstairs of a large house close to Casa Loma. Aarne's friend began work as a cook at the Brown Derby on Young Street, a popular restaurant, while Aarne wandered aimlessly, wondering what he should do. Sometimes he passed time in the movie theatre, or took in the steam baths.

Once, Aarne picked up his friend from the restaurant. The

50

streets were empty, so they strolled down the middle of the street toward their apartment like they owned the place. A police cruiser pulled up beside them.

"What are you doing out here at this hour?" The officer eyed them up and down.

"I just finished my shift at the Derby. We're on our way home," the Norwegian said. "We live over there." He pointed to a house down the avenue.

"Fine, but you shouldn't be walking in the middle of the street. The neighbours are nervous about two young men out here so late at night."

Aarne and his friend glanced at each other, but agreed with the officer. They'd be more careful, they promised.

Days and weeks passed. Aarne became restless. After several months some Finns told him about a great job opportunity. "You'll make great pay. The work is hard, but it's worth it," they said.

"Why not?" Aarne replied. There was nothing to keep him in Toronto. He went to a bush camp in Northern Ontario, close to Cochrane. Life in the bush was exhausting. Every night his body ached from the heavy work he was unaccustomed to doing and he'd sit by the cabin's heater, trying to sleep. When he managed a few hours, he was haunted by the terrors of his past. He was miserable. After a week, he'd had enough.

"Where are the big cities?" he asked one of the loggers. "I don't know where to go, but I don't want to stay here."

"There aren't any big cities like Toronto in the north, but Timmins and Sudbury are bigger than Cochrane, that's for sure," the man said.

"I like the sound of that name. Sudbury." He let the word roll off his tongue.

Aarne packed his meager belongings again and bought himself a ticket from Cochrane to North Bay where he would change the train to Sudbury. While he waited for the train from Montreal to arrive, a travelling salesman pulled his car up beside the platform.

"Anyone want a ride to Sudbury?" the salesman asked. He looked haggard. "I need someone to keep me awake for this last leg. I have a meeting in Sudbury in the morning, so I have to get there tonight."

Aarne suspected that the man was not only exhausted, but had been drinking, too. Despite his reservations, he decided to take his chances. "I'll go with you," he said, picking up his pack from the platform. He got into the car and the salesman expressed his gratitude.

After more than an hour on the road, the salesman pulled off the highway to get some coffee. "Welcome to Sudbury," he said.

Aarne looked around. There was a gas station that looked like a paper shed and very little else. "Jesus Christ, if this is Sudbury, bring me straight to the train station."

The salesman laughed. "Nah, I'm just kidding. We're in Coniston. We'll be in Sudbury soon."

Aarne was relieved, but wondered what lay ahead. The salesman dropped him off downtown at Radio Lunch across the street from Capitol Theatre on Durham. He grabbed something to eat at the restaurant and was relieved to see many other young people, some of them Finnish, at the establishment. He took his suitcase and headed toward some of the bigger buildings along Elm Street, wondering where he might find a room. When he heard his native language spoken by a couple of fellows, he asked for directions.

A Finnish woman named Sanna Hill rented rooms in a house at the corner of Regent and Elm, a stone's throw from the Court House. Here, other Finnish immigrants had found a space for themselves, and Aarne felt immediately at home.

He left his suitcase on the bed and strolled back into the heart of the town, toward *Vappaus*, the Finnish newspaper establishment that housed a coffee shop above it. Outside he struck up a conversation with some Finns.

"Where can I find some work around here?" Aarne asked.

"Do you paint?"

"I'm not a painter, but I can paint. I painted ships back home in Finland and Sweden," Aarne replied.

"Good. Be ready in the morning and I'll pick you up here at 8:00 AM. I have some contracts to paint houses in Lively." Aarne didn't know where Lively was, but he shook the man's hand and the next day Aarne started work.

Although he had a room and a temporary job, Aarne continued to look for better job opportunities. He applied for a job at Frood Mine, but after a few weeks working underground, he quit.

The sea continued to call, so he left Sudbury for Toronto, finding employment on a boat in the Great Lakes that shipped goods between Buffalo and Hamilton, and other American cities. When the company asked him to stay aboard the boat to take care of it during the off-peak winter months, Aarne decided a winter on board the lonely boat would be too long to endure, so he drifted back to Sudbury, finding work at the Copper Cliff smelter.

It wasn't long before the sea began to whisper to Aarne to return to her. He'd spent most of his time in Canada in Sudbury and had made many friends there, but he couldn't settle. This time, he booked a train to Vancouver, hoping to find work on a ship.

On his arrival in the port city, Aarne went straight to the sailors' union to inquire about job postings. "I'm an experienced sailor. Do you have anything for me?"

"There's a ship in North Vancouver looking for a man. It would suit you well," the union representative said. He gave Aarne the details.

Aarne pulled the piece of paper out of his pocket a few hours later and considered his options. He knew this would be a good job, but he'd never been to Vancouver and was eager to see more of the seaside city.

Eventually, Aarne needed work. He learned about a job opportunity in Northern British Columbia, building the hydro plant in Kitimat. It was an ambitious project. Aarne worked seven days a week with as much overtime as he wanted, earning two dollars an hour from his American employer, much more than Canadian employers paid. He spent the next eleven months working there and might have stayed longer, except for the news that a cross-country ski championship was coming to Northern Ontario. He marked his calendar with the day he needed to quit his job and board a train to Sudbury in time to see the races. He knew a famous Finnish skier would be racing, and he was determined to see him.

Aarne found himself back in the Northern town of Sudbury, with its many lakes and birch trees, a landscape that was reminiscent of his Northern Finnish home. Once again, he needed employment. He put on his work clothes, steel-toed boots, and hard hat and made his way to Copper Cliff where a smoke stack was being constructed for the iron plant.

"I'm ready to work," he said.

"I'm sorry, but we've hired too many people," the foreman said. Aarne was disappointed, but hung around all day, chatting to anyone who had some free moments. When lunchtime arrived, he sat down and ate a sandwich from his metal lunch box.

The next day, Aarne returned to the job site, dressed and ready. "What's your name?" the foreman asked, a little annoyed to see Aarne again.

"Kovala. Aarne."

"There's no work, Aarne. You might as well go home." Aarne nodded, but stayed on the jobsite, hoping the man would change his mind.

On the third day, Aarne arrived again, ready to work. The

foreman took one look at him and said, "Okay. I'd better hire you. I'll have to hire you anyway –" and shook his head, motioning Aarne to follow him.

One evening, Aarne decided to go to a dance at Sampo Hall on Antwerp Street. He abandoned his dirty work clothes and hard hat for a dark suit and tie, long overcoat, dress shoes, and fedora. The orchestra played waltzes and polkas from the small stage, and the dancers dressed in their Saturday best, their feet gliding against the wooden floor. Aarne spied a young woman across the hall. He combed his hair back between his fingers and strode across the crowded room to ask her to dance. She smiled up at the tall stranger.

Later, Aarne would learn that Anja Roiha, a young Finnish woman who grew up on a farm in rural Wanup, had always dreamed of marrying a sailor. Where she might find a sailor in farm country was beyond reckoning, but when she saw Aarne coming towards her across the hall, she said, "That's the man I'm going to marry."

Aarne's restlessness seemed to have settled down, but he told Anja he would never get married. Memories of the lives lost behind the Death Gate and during Death Marches made him question why he had survived when so many others had not.

For the next several years, while they dated, Aarne continued building smokestacks for Custodis, travelling to worksites all over Canada: from Vancouver to Brandon, Esterhazy to New Castle Bridge. Eventually, he revealed some of the horrific experiences he'd had in the concentration camp during the war to Anja. It was difficult for her to hear, and even more difficult for him to tell. His years of drifting from place to place, enjoying the complete freedom of having no ties, while never wholly escaping his terrible past, were making a more stable future desirable.

In October 1958, Aarne married Anja at the Finnish Lutheran Church on Mackenzie Street. Together, they travelled across the country, living in small town after small town as Aarne built smokestacks; twenty-four in total. They had two sons who travelled with them, but by the time the boys were ready to go to school, the couple decided it was time to finally settle down. They returned to the city they loved, Sudbury, to raise their family. Aarne's last chimney was Inco's Superstack, completed in 1972. By then he and Anja had a third son, and a daughter. Aarne continued to work in construction until he retired in 1988, building most of the city's major projects of the time, including Laurentian Hospital, City Centre Mall, and Laurentian University.

In 2012, at the age of eight-four, almost seventy years after the end of the war, Aarne was finally ready to share his experiences. For months he sat with his daughter, returning to the vivid memories of his past, the places that haunted his days and struck terror into his nights.

One morning, as she drove him to the Finnish bakery where the old-timers met every day, he said he'd woken with an intense headache and a pounding chest.

"I was in a ditch levelling concrete," he explained. "An SS officer came to the edge of the ditch and glared down at me. 'What are you doing?' the officer said in a commanding voice. Aarne glared up at the officer. 'Goddamn stupid. I'm levelling concrete.' He tightened the grip on his shovel. 'You can't touch me. Even if you are Hitler's brother, you can't touch me anymore.'"

Aarne was visibly shaken from the nightmare, but his voice revealed a touch of pride. He'd left his country as a young man to create a new life, find a purpose, an identity. He'd done everything he could to escape the prison the Nazis had created for his body and mind. Like the ever-changing sea, he allowed himself to float from one place to another until he found a safe harbour, returning time again to Sudbury, the northern community that he would eventually call home, and mooring himself to a place and a people he loved.

56

We Are the Undesirables
By Julio Heleno Gomes

For a cold December day the sun is blazing as bright as a ripe orange and the snow that came down overnight is layered like a soft blanket, branches of the broad evergreens drooping with clumps of ice and snow. Graders and sanders have been out and the twisting two-lane highway is scraped down to black pavement. Through the dull hours of this drive my companion Kingsley keeps nodding off, uninterested in small talk or observing the views the lonely road has to offer.

Our destination is Fort Frances, a town nestled on the north bank of the Rainy River, where Rainy Lake narrows and separates the state of Minnesota from Ontario. The fertile lowlands are dotted with timber-frame houses and crumbling, tin-roofed barns. Sometimes black-and-white cows can be spotted nuzzling around bales of hay. This is definitely farm country, but the area's beating heart is a sprawling pulp and paper mill, visible even from the overpass as you approach the town. A dizzying tangle of belt conveyors and mounds of wood shavings, pulp digesters and dryers, chip bins and blow tanks and bleaching towers, brick chimneys venting thick coils of exhaust into the lower atmosphere, the white smoke hanging in the crisp air like a landscape oil painting.

This is your typical blue-collar place and one thing is true: where there are good-paying jobs there's also a need to let off a different kind of steam, particularly as the work week draws to a close. The historic downtown hotel is a popular hangout and here to provide live entertainment, all the way from the Land of the Sleeping Giant, for a limited time only, will be Implicit Faith! The publicity photo pasted on the main doors may suggest the bad-boy attitude of the Rolling Stones and the effeminate menace of any hair metal band, but the reality is my friend and his colleagues are all now in their thirties, ordinary joes from Thunder Bay who pump out palatable rock music to a crowd that's only looking to cut loose, to forget the drudgery of their lives for a few hours in casual surroundings.

The gig at the undistinguished Rainy Lake Hotel ranks as a big deal for these guys. This is Implicit Faith's second time here as headliners, another four-day run. I tag along because I have vacation time to take and nowhere in particular to be, and since I once worked in the border area it's a trip down memory lane. I'm giving Kingsley a ride because my friend Henri, along with the bass player, went up the day before, his pickup truck crammed with the tools of their trade: guitars, amps, drum kit and accessories. The other two, guitarist and lead vocalist Dave and drummer Dano, will arrive in Dave's sedan—if it doesn't break down along the way.

Despite a name that evokes elegance mixed with frontier charm, the Rainy Lake Hotel's glory is clearly in the past, maybe as far back as when the voyageurs were portaging over ancient granite rock and through smothering wilderness. Its three-storey weathered brownstone facade still dominates a block of the downtown, situated next to family-run pharmacies, sandwich shops and native art galleries. Accommodations for touring bands are rarely luxurious—most are put up in rundown houses that are a step from being condemned—and even here the rooms are far from swanky. As band leader (meaning: manager, booking agent, accountant, driver, chief bottle washer), Henri's one prerogative is he gets the best of the slim pickings. On the outing in the summer he determined the "wood" room was the least objectionable of those held out by management. It boasts cheap 1970s wood panelling, double beds with lumpy mattresses and a scratched tub where the bathwater pools before reluctantly gurgling down the drain.

This is the nineteen-nineties and if you're a grizzled music journalist reflecting on the era you can be forgiven for believing this was the high-water mark for live, cutting-edge entertainment. A vibrant manufacturing economy still supported well-paying jobs, so club owners could count on a core of customers to keep coming through the doors. Into this fertile ecosystem went the go-getters with their heady dreams, coaxing rattletraps over the boundless highways of the Great White North. They were the reggae rockers, the screaming punks, the earnest folkies, the soulful chanteuses, the circus sideshow freaks, the in-your-face, let-it-all-hang-out types, for whom every dot on the map represented a chance to step under the lights and strut their stuff. Those were the pedestrian yet intoxicating Nineties before technology bestowed on us fifty-inch Plasma HDTVs, the 500-channel universe and round-the-clock Internet poker games—in-home entertainment which stuck its hooks into you, where you need not leave the hearth to get your dose of distraction.

But that was the digital tomorrow. In the here and now where everyone could singalong to Top-40 hits, a few dozen locals could be relied on to wander into the first-floor lounge, and between pitchers of watered-down draft beer and raucous games of billiards dutifully pause and turn to the guys flailing away on the low stage and holler the encouraging "woo-hoo, right on!" when Dave held a high note or Dano unleashed his sticks of fury on the crash and splash cymbals. Henri the guitarist and Slava the bassist are the mellow, unflashy ones, even when the group launches into frenzied renditions of favourites from Kiss, AC/DC or Guns N' Roses. Kingsley's post is at the back of the low-ceilinged room. Lord of the soundboard, his demure nature is overshadowed by constant fretting that the stack of Marshall amps aren't delivering the right kind of oomph. "They sound too thin," he mutters, tapping control knobs up and control knobs down, fastidiously turning buttons, every clanging note from the foursome requiring another adjustment, another tweak, all in the effort to make you believe it really could be Paul Stanley or Angus Young capering on the stage.

Rather than just lurk in the shadows and twiddle my thumbs I volunteer to preside over the lighting desk, freeing Kingsley to obsess over feedback and reverb. The lights operate on a basic system where I punch buttons on a board which wink the blue, green, yellow and red bulbs in the rack over the stage, producing a kaleidoscopic blur of colours that I worry I'm overdoing and might induce epileptic fits. I don't know that I added anything to the show, but I did try to time the flashing hues to peak moments, such as when Henri was doing Ted Nugent-style backbends as he scratched the whammy bar across the guitar strings or when Dave was comically stammering through a BTO tune. No extra charge for that, folks.

The engagement consists of a four-day run, two shows a night, starting at ten o'clock and ending by last call. The only noteworthy mishap occurred early on when Dave's voice suddenly cracked and he could barely manage a croak, leading a wag in the cheap seats to grumble that "this band sucks!" After a hasty huddle, they re-arranged the set list and Henri stepped to the mike for a few songs until Dave's vocal chords were sufficiently recovered to resume primary vocal duties.

Together now for several years, the foursome has developed an undeniable chemistry and while they may not have the technical proficiency and fun-time stage presence of Bob Seger and his brilliant bandmates, when they're on stage and in the spotlight they give it their all; it truly does feel to them like they're a million miles away.

If a few people dance and a few applaud it's worth the effort because Implicit Faith have reached the summit and breathed rarefied air. When they step off the stage for the last time they feel like conquering heroes, high-fives all around. Afterward it's a gentle descent from the adrenaline rush. The guys hold down day jobs so partyin' till the break of dawn isn't their thing anymore. Besides, boozing now leads to longer-lasting hangovers and a literal blow to the gut when the pay packet is finally opened.

This commitment was never regarded as a holiday, so getting up before noon wasn't a violation of some rocker's twisted code of conduct. What, then, to do with all those hours before the clocked bidded them on stage to crank out the tunes? In anticipation of so much free time, Henri and I had decided, perhaps in the throes of school-boy optimism, to pack skates, winter boots, hockey sticks, pucks and tennis balls for what would surely be carefree scrimmages at a nearby rink. What is more Canadian than a hard-working bar band playing scrub hockey in their downtime? Like most honourable intentions, it never came to pass.

With nothing much to occupy the daytime hours, we'd wander the streets, but since there were only a couple of blocks of shops—the downtown being hemmed in by the mill complex and the river—the novelty rapidly wore off. The routine was to dip into a sandwich shop, buy the largest item on the menu, eat half of it and save the rest for dinner or a late-night snack. The other guys would lounge around their rooms watching TV and smoking cigarettes or walk to the riverfront to ponder the water as it slid by or contemplate if life on the American side is really so much different from our own.

We all did gather for a meal once, in the hotel's restaurant, a room that could've served as a saloon in a old west flick. It was lunchtime, which for musicians means a late breakfast, so the orders were eggs, bacon and omelettes, clubhouse sandwiches, fries not onion rings and, thanks, but no gravy, because that costs a few more cents. Henri, whose only employment at this time was orchestrating the rise of this world-beating band, was hard up for cash so Dave and I picked up his tab, which he kept to a minimum by drinking water instead of non-stop cups of coffee. The waitress, a local girl who was not yet jaded about the daily grind of taking orders and carting plates of greasy burgers and fries to impatient customers, was congenial, hovering about us like a mother hen, not in expectation of a large tip I'm guessing but merely for the fact the six of us could be regarded as something out of the ordinary: a group of strangers from the big city, and musicians to boot! No doubt she'd have giddy stories to tell of her encounters with honest-to-goodness rock 'n' rollers. But likely the most lasting impression belongs to us: being the chatty Cathy-type she managed to puncture our fantasies that she was star-struck when she came by during her innumerable rounds to top up the cups of java and casually remarked, "You know, you guys are the cheapest band I've seen around here." Taking it as less than lofty praise, Henri and I frowned. It was up to Dave, the merriest member of the band, to step to the fore and inquire as to the meaning of her statement. You're frugal, she opined, because other bands that play here put all kinds of meals and phone calls on their bill, which means they sometimes end up getting nothing from their stay. As I raised the coffee mug to my lips, I winked at Henri, thinking, well, that means Implicit Faith are smart businessmen not fools.

Of course, as we were leaving we dug in our pockets for dollar bills, dimes and quarters to ensure the tip was generous enough not to bring scorn on our name.

Across the deep river is Fort Frances's American counterpart, International Falls, an even more unassuming town which conversely blazes like a beacon for Canadian shoppers, the low exchange rate no hindrance to the seemingly one-way flow of traffic. On our third day Henri announces he's so bored he's taken to counting how much time passes before a pigeon perches on the eaves of the building across the way. He needs batteries for his wireless transmitter, so we inform the others of our plan and get into my Eagle Talon to venture across the border, "just a hop from Port John to Port Jill," as he terms it. It is a short trip, rattling through the mill grounds and over a concrete two-lane toll bridge that spans the river as it makes a hard turn over a set of shale rapids. (There's a central section for heavy trucks and rail cars because the Boise Cascade company, which actually owns the bridge, has operations on both sides of the river that necessitate regular crossings, the U.S.-Canada divide being merely a mythical barrier.)

Sometimes I'm as squishy as a jellyfish in the presence of authority figures, so the trip is undertaken with nervousness on my part. I was born in Portugal and only as an adult did I obtain Canadian citizenship, reckoning that a blue passport decorated with red maple leaves would invite scant scrutiny when trying to enter the United States. For young people, it is almost a rite of passage that when you attain your age of majority you confidently walk into a bar to order your first legal drink, and though that limit is higher in the States a similar celebration is de rigueur for northerners, meaning a pilgrimage to the American end of Lake Superior, where cheap booze is almost enshrined in the Constitution. That wasn't the reason I became a Canadian citizen in 1983, but it certainly didn't hurt the following year when I was assigned to an extra gang on the railway. The crew spent the summer doing grunt work in various locations to the west of Thunder Bay, mostly in the Rainy River district, all the way to where the Manitoba and Ontario boundaries meet the northern edge of Minnesota at Lake of the Woods. In the off-hours, some of the guys would cross the border to shoot pool and pound back Miller High Lifes at the first taphouse they came to, for no reason other than to say they'd done something unique.

That was plucking fruit from the tree of opportunity. The disquieting part was earlier when a car full of young men approached the isolated border crossing and were subject to the stern gaze of border agents who knew just about everyone in these parts and would welcome a change from the routine: to vex a vehicle packed with young men, some of whom likely had had brushes with the law in their unruly teenage years, some of whom had blithely forgotten they had packets of dried up weed stashed in the glove box. But since we all seemed to be good Canadian boys from a staid Canadian city not too far away, just working in the area for the time being and with some of that funny Canuck money to burn, we were waved through after sweating it for a while.

It's midday as Henri and I pull up to the U.S. customs booth on the other side of the bridge. The car glides to a gentle stop, I roll down the window and, knowing how these things work, present my winningest smile. It suddenly begins to crumble. This border officer must've trained with the KGB for no human emotion sullies his face as he regards us. Where you from? Where you going? he asks in a bored tone, studying Henri's driver's licence and my passport. Going to do some shopping, we answer. OK, park the car over there and go inside that building.

Henri and I say nothing, as if this is perfectly normal. Oh, boy, I'm thinking, this adventure is off to a flying start. How will it end?

I steer the car, a low-slung burgundy-coloured coupe that looks flashier than its anemic four-cylinder engine actually performs, towards the administration building. I park it, we get out, straighten our jackets, run a comb through our hair and march inside, a stiff winter breeze pushing us forward. We sit on a long black leather

64

bench, hands on our knees like penitents awaiting a session with the father confessor. Behind the counter, two male officers shuffle about to no obvious purpose, occasionally directing cool glances our way, while another one jabs his index fingers on a keyboard, squints at a computer screen and peers at our documents. We are untroubled and exude Buddha-like serenity, for we know nothing disconcerting will pop up in their records, for we are choirboys.

When we are summoned, it's another round of interrogation. Whatcha doin' in the States? Um, gonna do some shoppin', maybe get a bite to eat, we respond in a relaxed manner. After questions about where we're from, why we're there, why we're in Fort Frances, from a back office emerges another one, shorter and rounder than his colleagues, a presence no one can ignore. As he struts by empty desks his right arm is swinging, as if magnetically drawn to the .40-calibre pistol strapped to his hip.

"So, whatcha boys doin' in the States?" he says to us after sidling up to the counter to stand by his buddies, oozing faux friendliness.

Why are we here? Why does anyone from Canada come to this wondrous place?

"We just wanted to go to the States," I answer cheerfully.

"Well," he replies, "ya are in the States."

Henri and I look blankly at each other. Well, then, I wanted to blurt out, it's been a lotta fun. Guess we'll be heading back now. Thank you kindly.

Instead, knowing that would be an ill-advised retort—because the ploy is so obviously to rattle us—through gritted teeth we mumble about shopping and eating, seeing the sights.

"Ever been charged with a criminal offence?" he asks. Charged, not convicted, you will notice.

No, sir, we respond soberly.

"You bringing in any fruits, vegetables, agricultural products?"

We're taken aback but a timid No comes from our lips.

"Bringing any money with you?"

Yes, sir. A few dollars, not much, for shopping and lunch."That your car? Can we have the keys please?"

I hand over the key ring. Two of them tramp out. The hardy kind, they don't bother with outerwear. Through the high windows we see them squeeze into the small vehicle, peer under the seats, inspect the ash tray, paw through the glove compartment, then roll out and circle to the back. The hatch is flung open and they shake a cardboard box, looking to uncover God knows what; it holds an ice scrapper, snow brush and a jug of windshield washer fluid. A hockey stick with a plastic blade is shoved aside and they peer in a plastic Zellers bag, examining the hiking boots I still haven't put on my feet. Then one begins tapping the panel of the hatch, running his hand along the edge, then he lifts up the carpet and checks the well where the donut spare sits, along with the tire iron and lug wrench.

Henri is biting his lip, his hands thrust in the pockets of his jacket, his head of extravagant blond curls obscuring the rest of his face. I'm standing, swaying from the shoulders, a dumb grin on my face, admiring the shiny lights in the ceiling, wondering if my car's going to be impounded.

"OK, boys, here you go," one of them says at last, placing the keys on the counter. "You have a nice day now."

We passed the test!

We don't feel relief though we express perfunctory gratitude to, you know, be allowed to enter the magical land of America and this picturesque corner of paradise. Sheesh! My Italian pals would've left with a hearty and enigmatic, "*Che cavolo!*"

With an irrational notion that a multitude of eyes are focused on us, we trudge back to the car. As we pull away we are wary they might spring one last surprise and unleash shrieking hounds and steel-helmeted troopers, so we are silent as I maneuver down a block of shiny gas stations, antique shops and seedy bars, then out towards the retail zone, expecting at any moment a sheriff's patrol car and flashing roof lights to fill the rearview mirror.

But nothing happened. We spent a few hours listlessly walking through stores, our enthusiasm and appetite greatly dulled. There was a Kmart and Henri did purchase nine-volt batteries, enough to power his electric guitars through a thousand versions of Stairway to Heaven.

On the way back we prowled pass the U.S. customs building, wondering if the guards were still keeping an eye out for undesirables such as us. As we neared the Canada Border Services station at the other end of the bridge, the Maple Leaf looking so welcoming as it fluttered on a pole, we come up to a line of pickup trucks. I strum my fingers on the steering wheel and breathe a sigh of relief. The Canada customs officer is a young woman, which puts me in good spirits even as she peppers us with the routine questions of where we're from, how long have we been out of the country, what is the total value of all the goods we're bringing back? Henri complies by presenting his bulging bag of nine-volt batteries, total cost declared to the penny, in U.S. currency, the sales slip clutched in his hand for instant verification. Then she asks me to pop the hatch on the car. She emerges from her booth and shuffles around the car. I notice she does not carry a sidearm. I hear her rummaging among the clutter in the back.

"You have brand-new boots here," she declares, holding up a plastic shopping bag with the red letters of the popular home-grown retailer. "Do you have a receipt for these?"

I turn to a stone-faced Henri, then peer at her over the back seat. "No," I say. "I bought those weeks ago in Thunder Bay. At the Zellers. That's why they're still in the Zellers bag. I brought them to play road hockey. That's why there's a hockey stick, puck and balls back there."

150 YEARS UP NORTH AND MORE

"Well, these are brand new. You should have a store receipt," she replies.

"I didn't know I wasn't going to use them and I didn't remember they were there when we decided to go across to the U.S. for an afternoon drive," I say, an edge creeping into my voice.

She closes the hatchback and returns to her booth. She resumes her seat and says nothing as she scribbles on a paper. Without looking up she hands us our identification.

"There you go," she says curtly. "Have a nice day."

I drive the car down the concrete ramp and around a corner as we emerge in the mill property, bouncing over a spider's web of railroad tracks, dodging pulp trucks rumbling to and from the laydown yard. I turn on to the main street, eager for the sanctuary of the faded hotel.

We loafed about in our room the rest of the day, Henri sitting on the edge of the bed, leaning over an acoustic guitar, playing melancholy chords from the Neil Young songbook. I sit in a chair by the window thumbing through a dense and forgettable novel, often looking across the street to count pigeons. When it was time to go down to the lounge and prepare for the final night, we are the first to arrive. The rest of the band filters in and they each attend to their duties, tuning instruments, ensuring every cord is plugged in, Kingsley adjusting knobs on the soundboard while I ponder the rudimentary lighting desk, hoping new features had mysteriously been added, a magic button to send forth fireworks like it was Canada Day.

At the first thunderous strains of drums, cymbals and duelling guitars, the rack of lights explode like a supernova. The modest crowd gave a half-hearted cheer, the boys ploughed on, trying to settle into a groove. As the night wore on, more and more locals drift in and the noise in the lounge rises to an audible buzz, bursts of energy dulling the noise coming from the amplifiers, yet Henri and his company keep plugging away, accepting the energy flowing about them, capturing it and harnessing it. They were so in synch that the evening passed in a blur, the well-trodden songs soaring to a new level of enjoyment and satisfaction, as happily happens on Saturdays. Later, after the obligatory two-song encore, the last note from the guitars, the last clang of the cymbals having faded into the quiet night, the guys gather at a table for the ritual of raising a beer to celebrate the finale, the most successful show, everyone too exhausted and contemplative to engage in conversation, as if speaking would break the magic spell.

"You guys won't believe what happened to us today," I finally said, and hearing no dissent I launched into a recital of our encounter with U.S. Customs and Border Protection that morning, trying to spin our adventure into a humorous yarn.

When I finished the telling, Slava, the most reserved of the bunch, lowered the glowing cigarette from his lips. "That happened to us, too," he said and exhaled.

Henri and I looked disbelievingly at each other, ready to guffaw. But since Slava was a man of few, yet wise words, this was a statement that had to be taken seriously.

So, to rewind. Henri and I decide to go across the border, leaving Dave, Dano and Slava on their own, but having planted an idea that would take root. "What are we gonna do? Maybe we can go across as well," Dave explains of their discussion. Off they go in Dave's ramshackle Hyundai Pony (Korea's First Car!), an ugly sedan your grandmother uses for grocery shopping. Surprisingly, it doesn't raise eyebrows with the border guards, but Slava's long curly black hair, leather jacket and stylishly torn jeans probably do, as does Dano's admission of law-breaking when he was a minor. Dave, the strait-laced Randy Bachman-figure in the band, is left to cool his heels while the other two get to go under the interrogation lamp. Dano and Slava's aw-shucks, little-boy-lost genuineness probably exhausted the American Gestapo agents and after several hours they were finally deemed harmless and were allowed to proceed onto the land of the free and the home of the brave.

The ordeal was hardly worth it.

"I don't think we spent more than fifteen or twenty minutes in that town," Dave relates. "There was nothing to see or do."

The excitement and expectation of the trip was no doubt blunted by grim-faced officialdom, so the longed-for journey to a sleepy border town commenced with a sour taste in the mouth. I knew the sensation all too well.

"We didn't buy a single thing," Dave announces.

"Not even a chocolate bar," Slava adds.

Shaking my head and chuckling in sympathy, I turn to Henri, whose blue eyes were twinkling while the story was unfolding.

"Well, what did you think of that?" I ask, daring him to say our hassles were small potatoes compared to what the others had endured.

"Holy frig," he said slowly, "those batteries sure were cheap."

Weddings
1923 aug 24.

LEE—CHURCH

One of the prettiest weddings of the season was solemnized at the United Church, Callander, on Tuesday, when Florence May, youngest daughter of Mr. and Mrs. William Church, became the bride of Alfred W. Lee, son of A. Lee, of Bracebridge, and the late Mrs. Lee. The ceremony was conducted by the Rev. D. Bishop before a bell shaped background of white bloom, while a profusion of lovely roses and garden blossoms completed the pretty altar decoration. To the strains of Mendelssohn's wedding march, played by Miss Bessie Duncan, the winsome bride entered the church escorted by her brother-in-law, B. Shannon. She wore a French frock of Elizabeth crepe, heavily embroidered with crystal beads, and her veil was worn in cap effect with a coronet of orange blossoms. The bridal bouquet was a shower of Ophelia roses and maiden fern. The maid of honor, Miss Eileen Rayner, was daintily gowned in mauve silk crepe with canary yellow trimmings, and wore a large hat to match, with trimmings of rhinestones. She carried a bouquet of sweetheart roses. Aubrey Lee, brother of the bridegroom, was best man and Edward Quinn ushered the guests to their places. During the signing of the register, Mrs. David McNulty sang "Until." Following the ceremony, a dainty buffet luncheon was served at the home of the bride's parents to the immediate friends of the happy couple. Later on Mr. and Mrs. Lee left for their home in Bracebridge, the bride travelling in a pheasant brown satin dress with coat to match and small felt hat in rosewood shade. Among the out-of-town guests for the wedding were Mr. and Mrs. A. Church, Mrs. H. Rousseau, of Nipissing, Miss Eileen Rayner, Mrs. Franklin Reid and H. Broomhead, of North Bay.

History of Small Handed Women
By Susan Eldridge-Vautour

History is organized neatly into words and phrases, in ink, on paper. The unruly jumble of photographs, journals and newspaper clippings in my large steamer trunk resists such treatment. My mind struggles to find a narrative thread to pull them into order. I think of embroidery floss, strands of DNA and meandering rivers.

In a wedding designed for a debutant, Florence Church became Florence Lee. At 25, she was old for a bride but beautiful nonetheless, dressed in Elizabeth crepe and crystal beads. On my bedroom wall, I have a photograph of her in the bow of a canoe. In it, she is turned and smiling. I have her tiny hands, passed along first to my mother and now to me. I love to propel our canoe forward while my husband winds us around boulders in fast moving water. Growing up, Florence's handiwork included needlepoint and piano. Nothing in her cultivated upbringing prepared her for the life she marched into during that gorgeous summer ceremony in August of 1925.

According to my mother's handwritten memories, things started off well enough. Alfred and Florence had a farm in Bracebridge where my mom, Alice, was born in 1927. They sold the farm and bought a small house in Toronto where Alfred worked construction during the day and took blueprint reading courses at night.

Along with almost everyone else, the 1929 depression knocked them off balance and swept them away. Alfred lost his job and the house. By then, Alice had a younger brother, Dave. She loved him fiercely but couldn't help but be jealous. One of her enduring memories was of being a young girl in the churchyard, listening as Alfred introduced Dave as his "first born". Of course he meant first born son, but my mom knew then that girls didn't really count.

Alfred rented a rundown bungalow that had a decently sized yard in which he planted a vegetable garden and flower beds. The place was greatly improved and so the landlord raised the rent. It must have pained them deeply to have to go on relief.

In 1934, a fire devoured the entire town of Callander and Florence's mother's big rooming house was the last to go up. All that was saved was some of the furniture and the barn. A small cottage was built in which my great grandmother lived out the rest of her days. When she died, she left the place to Florence.

In 1936, Florence and Alfred, Alice and Dave, and now little Oliver, squeezed into the cramped quarters. Alfred received a bequest from a distant English relative and added an upstairs and a summer kitchen. The furniture finally came in from the barn. I imagine that the beautiful "secretary" desk that my mother treasured her whole life and that now sits in my bedroom was one of those rescued pieces. I should dust it more often.

There were no jobs in Callander so Alfred travelled to find work doing logging or construction. He sent letters and money home from Heron Bay, Mink Lake and Kapuskasing. Florence would get used to being on her own and then Alfred would return. She'd get used to having him home and he'd leave again. It was a hard life but it was preferable to asking for relief.

In all, Florence had five children: Alice, Dave, Oliver, Mona and Phyllis. My mom's recollections are recorded in her atrocious handwriting in a cheap purple note pad and I also have some recent letters from my Aunt Phyllis. She has fond memories of building forts in the bush and playing make believe. I know that my Uncle Oliver struggled under Alfred's strict rules and brutal consequences. Only Mona and Phyllis remain and I am as bad at visiting as I am at dusting.

Callander had only a small library, certainly, but Alice read the entire library by the time she was six and finished grade 10 at fourteen, having skipped a couple of grades along the way. She was undeniably intelligent and wanted to continue onto grade 11 but that would have meant taking a bus into North Bay at a cost of ten dollars per month. Alice begged and pleaded to no avail. In 1941, it was considered wasteful and possibly unwise to waste education on a girl. She was already too smart for her own good.

Instead, Alice was hired out as a mother's helper for two dollars per week plus her keep. It was bad enough that she had to sleep with the children, one of whom wet the bed, but when they demanded that she take the kids to the midway on her day off, Alice quit. Being that the minister had gotten her the job, she quit church too and never went back.

There was little chance that she'd get another job in town so she put an ad in the Domestic Service section of the *Toronto Star* and she received hundreds of replies. Because of the war, the women who had been housekeepers were now at factory work but Alice was too young for that. In order to be properly employed one needed a National Registry card which could be applied for at sixteen. Alice was only fourteen years old when she carefully folded a few clothes and some of the more promising responses to her ad into her small suitcase and boarded the train to Toronto. Before too long, her value as domestic servant increased to fifteen dollars per week plus board and she felt well off.

Alice was proud to spend a great deal of her earnings on Christmas presents for her family back home, where they had moved from Callander to Widdifield Station. She pictured a station with sidewalks and roads in various directions but what she found, when she finally made it north, was a bush path. Alice ruined her new shoes and a pair of silk stockings by walking through the mud and snow but when she got in, her siblings gave her wool socks for her feet and a warm cup of cocoa for her belly.

In June 1943, Alice finally turned sixteen and Florence accompanied her to North Bay city hall to apply for all-important NR card. Shortly afterward, Alice got a "real" job closer to home and Florence had a spectacular breakdown.

Surely moving into a house that had been used for years to keep chickens might have had something to do with it. Those delicate hands scraped layers of chicken poop off every surface, carefully cleaning out every crevice. How she must have hated that house. It was very hot the day that Florence tried to burn it down with everyone inside of it. Fortunately, the coal oil she sprayed all over the attic turned out to be only DDT. That was when Alfred decided to have her put away. She had been manic, on and off, for some time: unsettled and agitated. Initially, Alfred tried to send her to stay with her family but she refused to stay put. Florence spent the rest of her life institutionalized, first at Mimeco in Toronto and then in the psychiatric hospital north of North Bay. Alice visited weekly at first, then monthly, then sporadically, then not at all. She never forgave herself for abandoning her mother but it was simply too depressing (and there was always that irrational fear that someone might decide that Alice belonged there too). Florence died before I was born but I have her tiny hands and I try to be strong (I try not to be too crazy).

75

Alice carried on, as people do. At a rate of about $30 a week she was able to live pretty well. She took the train to Toronto almost every weekend to shop and go to shows and she started dating her friend's brother, Sonny. One night she was late to meet him at the factory where he worked and he left without her. My father, Tom Eldridge, happened by and she married him in 1946. The ceremony was nothing like her parents' but it was equally transformative. Like Florence, Alice was utterly unprepared for what married life would bring.

Alice and Tom lived with his parents in Toronto until the night Tom punched his father in the mouth. Tom rented a room and then left Alice "forever" for the first time. Alice hated the room and immediately gave notice. She also packed Tom's lunch, just in case he came back. He did come back, the next morning and was glad that she had given notice but furious that she'd made his lunch.

Tom ran around on Alice from the start and spent all the money he was meant to be saving for a down payment on a house. Alice got pregnant. Tom got arrested. My oldest sister, Patty, was born while Tom was in jail. When he got out, Tom started work right away, roofing or painting. He was terribly sick after his first day out of jail—it could have been sunstroke or perhaps the horseradish was off. Maybe honest work just didn't agree with him. He soon went back to jail for punching out a guy in the hotel lobby who was standing around looking like he owned the place—turned out, he did.

Alice went on welfare which was enough to buy milk and food for Patty. Alice didn't eat as well as she should have which is likely why my mom had false teeth for as long as I can remember. This time when Tom got out of jail, he worked nights at one restaurant and she worked days at another. In spite of this incompatible schedule, Alice got pregnant again and Tom went to jail, again. This time he and a buddy had robbed a truck so he was off to Kingston penitentiary. Alice wound up with 3 children: Patty, Charlie and Lynn before he went away for a longer stint. My mom fondly remembered her years in the north raising my three siblings, without my father, as some of her best. It's hard to understand why Alice would have ever taken Tom back after 10 peaceful years apart, but she did, and I was born in 1966. Shortly afterward, my father really did leave my mother forever so it was just me and my mom.

Amongst my papers I have my parents' divorce document. It names me—a bright, four year old girl—as the child of the marriage. My father was served in jail and he never contested. In fact, years later, he described the day he signed the papers releasing my mother from her vows: "...and so this broad comes in with her fancy leather briefcase and asks if I considered your mom a fit parent. I said to the broad with the briefcase, 'did you hear that steel door clanging behind you on the way in? And you want my opinion of whether she's a fit parent?! Now that's rich.'" It is rich, but it was 1970 and women's rights hadn't really taken hold. Throughout school, I was often the only kid from a "broken" home.

Alice was a wonderful mother to me. She crafted a world full of love and magic. Her small hands seemed always to be picking berries or kneading bread or strumming a guitar.

I think we have a strand now, let me draw it through the eye of a tiny silver needle and stitch together layers of fabric. Is it Florence's French frock or perhaps her floral print hospital gown? I suppose we'll use both. There is Alice's pale blue cotton tee, worn inside out because the seams irritated her skin. Being a little more flamboyant, I have been known to rock a red sundress over bare legs so I will draw the thread through this as well.

Still, any fabric will unravel if you tug long enough at a frayed edge. We, all three, have unravelled now and then. Florence wound up locked away when she fell apart. Alice had bouts of neurosis when she'd believe herself infested with some kind of bug. She'd self administer toxic chemical treatments to rid herself of the fictional infestation. I remember spending weeks with my sister's family while my mom pulled herself back together.

At fifty years old, I really try not to pick at loose threads, keeping my own hands busy at other things: endless meals, child care, this keyboard.

My mom died over ten years ago now and I still miss her most days. My husband, Scott, reminds me of her in many ways which may be why we get along so well after 25 years of marriage. There was no notice in any newspaper of our country wedding. I wore blue cotton tie dye and we held hands as we walked into a circle of our family and friends. He has huge hands, my husband, and he takes good care of me. We live on the Vermillion River in a big, beautiful house and, together, we have raised three boys into young men. The river flows by fast in the spring and freezes in the winter. We swim and fish and canoe.

From my place at the front of our canoe, I turn often to smile at my husband. Like my mother, he likes nothing better than fishing for trout in cold, brown rivers. Sometimes, I look down into the water and see my reflection cast back. Mostly, I look like my father—Tom's strong cheek bones and jaw but then I look at the paddle in my small hands and I remember who I am.

A Minnow Catcher
By Caitlin Sylvia McAuliffe

Colourful cedar wood cabins sit quietly in dark blues, faded yellows and mint green; saunas perched between pinched cliffs; boats tucked into their boathouses rock on the water. Toasted pine needles caught on faded window ledges; the honeyed sun pours in, warming outstretched pages in books. Someone cracks open a beer, bubbles fizz to the top; liquid that looks like caramel. *Suola kala* is passed around on a ceramic plate: a thick slab of butter spread on homemade bread, cured salmon pressed with pieces of salt.

This is how I know it. Lake Panache.

Cutting holes in barren sheets of ice to drop a fishing line, or dash in, racing from the sauna. Climbing snowy granite rock cliffs, pretending we are mountaineers; eating salty potato chips under forts made of tree branches, throwing off sweaty mittens. We watch our parents pull the fish hut by a rope like a child with a sleigh, while Ma says, "you should have kids while you're young. I am sure glad we did. That way you can be kids with them".

Tucked between life jackets and towels in the tiny front cubby of the boat we clamour and coo until we're pulled out and carried to the cabin like bundles of firewood. In July's fervour we eat soda crackers from the box and French braid our hair, tickling bronzed backs from the scorching sun until an easy sleep falls upon us.

In the night my Mummu peels our tiny bodies from our mattress that lays on the floor to lead us to the lake for a cool dip. The air is warm, our sheets wrapped up in our feet, sweating and moist. Like a goose with her goslings, hands clasped to one another, her sheer turquoise housecoat floats behind her like a gypsy's cloak, opal patterns tread across the sky, the milky moon luminous. With heavy eyelids we trickle down the steps of the silvered dock and submerge our bodies. Tiny specs devoured by a vast, dark blue we wet our sun-stroked skin like shoreside stones in the plunge of midnight, stars ablaze; they flicker and spit like lit matches tossed into a firebox, feverish sparks that growl and snarl as they claw at tinder in the blackness.

Fog arises with morning's lull, a line perched between a fisherwoman's palm, nimble yet on guard; a beast tangled in the line, the boat rattles and rocks. My Mummu is laughing loudly, flailing her arms to the sky, she gushes and brags until the day breaks. I see how Finnish women wear nothing on their face.

She tells us about Great Mummu, Sylvia Maki. I know her already. Through words, echoed stories, black and white photographs that I crinkle in my hands hundreds of times over. Rising at dawn with paddle at hand, canoe as vessel, Great Mummu would slip into the creek, a mist rising behind jagged pines, cradling smooth white birch. She is a Minnow Catcher, you know. She also milked dairy cows and was almost struck by lightning twice on the Maki Farm.

The Beaver Lake newspaper states, "Sylvia and Eino Maki received their first minnow licence in 1949 and have helped provide fishermen [and fisherwomen] with bait for more than

30 years." Their red barn could be spotted alongside Highway 17 tucked behind cattails and brown meadows, "Live Minnows" painted in bold white on its side, a familiar landmark for locals. Minnow Maki, they would say.

With the flick of her wrist and net by her side, Great Mummu would scoop slippery grey minnows in her aluminum bucket while Great Papa would do the sales mingling. She was solitary and preferred to bury herself deep in the landscapes; the lakes or rivers or the back trails in the woods.

Picking blueberries from the branch, the sun blisters naked shoulders, the scratchy bush roughs at ankles, mosquitoes buzzing, a horse fly bites at flesh. Blueberries are heaving, melting like hot pie in the sun, sweet sugar that hangs like dusk; *magic*. My basket slowly fills to a purply blue, my fingers stained, dew glinting in the light. I think mostly of her.

Stubborn as a mule, one winter she said she would cross country ski 100 times alone on the bush trail. "We thought she was crazy," my Mummu puffs, "but she did it." Another time, Mummu went searching for her because she never came home.

"I drove at dusk to the creek, her station wagon was still parked and there she was, giddy and pulling up her green canoe. She said she had "got distracted" my Mummu says with a scolding tone and yet, a shining grin.

She was married to the lake.

Our little house sits beside the railway line in Whitefish. It rattles in the night, the familiar boom of the track, the steel clanks and hums, the train sounds its strained horn. My dog, who was once a stray, is tucked at the foot of my bed. I wiggle my toes under his warm, lanky body. Whitefish: our tucked up town sits right beside Beaver Lake, the rural FinnTown my Mummu grew up in.

150 YEARS UP NORTH AND MORE

"Why did you guys come to Northern Ontario, Mummu?"
"Because they said it looked just like Finland" she replies. Meanwhile the CPR was being built and the lumberyards offered work. My Mummu tells me she met my Papa at a barn dance, growing up on the farm. "I didn't want to marry a Finlander," she says. My Papa is Dutch. They came to own Whitefish Shell Service Station, later called Bert's Auto: a mechanic shop, roadhouse and gas station. For some time they lived in the one room apartment aside it, sliding out of bed with two kids to put on fresh pots of steaming coffee and roll open the wide garage doors, floor jacks holding up rusty automobiles, cement walls lined with tools; ratchets, pliers and wrenches set neatly in their place, their pet dog slinking behind the cash counter.

Mummu conversed with locals, passersby, bear hunters shuffling through for the Fall Hunt; grabbing at their coffee at morning rush hour, picking thick sliced ham and cheese sandwiches neatly wrapped in plastic wrap, and plopping them into their tin lunch boxes or exhausting her famous pies, wiping them clean from the bakery window. Mummu would lead the girls, a staff of ten bumbling in full skirts and loud voices. Papa would learn everything by hand to run the mechanic shop, having left Holland at the age of 17 with young memories of WWII, when butter was a high commodity. Working previously picking tobacco in Southern Ontario, and then for Department of Highway doing rounds in winter as a snowplow driver. He would talk thoughtfully with grease stained hands in his blue coveralls, handing us a Juicy Fruit gum right from his pocket. When we would visit, he never raised his voice; his company and the room would always be homely and light.

Down the road locals would bumble in and out of the rickety Lake Panache Hotel at all hours of the day. They'd sit at a bar for a drink aside the town's long haired drunk or a sleepy hitchhiker headed West. They'd dance long into the night with a woman dressed as a man, her thin hands giving her away.

In Winter, outlanders would trickle from bootlegger to bootlegger along the snowmachine trail or wrap a bladder of wine along their waist, hugging the inside of their snowmachine jacket; guzzling it midway, passing it around, helmets propped on foreheads. With kids, they would straddle them in sleighs or boats. In summer blood, gutsy teenagers jump off The Black, from a heavy rope hanging from the railway trestle into a restless set of rapids at Centennial Park. While the lesser, sit at The Point, a long dipped rock near the boat launch, or swim to The Pier: a crumbling platform that once stood as a steadfast pillar for the train, climbed by using a shambly wooden ladder to unabashedly jump from 20 feet high.

Fisherpeople float by on McCharles Lake in their aluminum boats, fishing rods linked to their side, sifting through their tackle box like at a candy store, comparing cherry red jigs, spinners and bottom bouncers, shiny toothed hooks dressed in pink frills and dangles. And by the tracks, a quaint post office sits, we'd bike there for two caramel candies every week.

This was all before they would reroute the highway and the buzzing would become desolate; roaring transports would disappear and stores would put up their closing signs. Beaver Lake and Whitefish would shrink and the working class would migrate to the city or to the next closest town. But the bumbling on the lakes would never cease and the ladder atop the pier would continue to be climbed over and over again.

There is an oddity about minnows: Small European freshwater fish common in gravelly streams or lakes. All this time I had seen minnows, tagged them to a hook, but I had never been a Minnow

Catcher, never canoed aside a school of minnows, like Great Mummu. I watch them instead, lying on my belly at the dock. I watch them swarm, swim in schools, side by side, like geese flying under water in a v-shaped formation; the same synchronicity. It is both noticeable and curious that when minnows are threatened they huddle closer together, fly after another; left to centre, right to centre, like braiding a rope. They rarely flee. It would be pronouncing death, otherwise. Reliance always inherits safety. A freshwater species living in schools, much like a family. A common minnow. Perhaps that is us too.

"Oh no!" my Ma yells, "Did she spit it out?" My Dad is pulling up the line with bare hands, mitts astrew, ski pants hanging at his waist, knee-deep in the snow aside the open fishing hole. The line releases abruptly, "Damn!" he mutters tumbling to the cushion of his elbows. The next time he quickens his pace, hand over hand, hand over hand. Noticing the fish arriving at the surface about to spit out the hook, he throws his fist into the icy water; grabbing the pike by her gills, he springs backwards as her fins tear into the flesh of his palm. Bloodying the snow around them, she gulps for breath. The hook in my dad's skin, left intact.

Panache Lake becomes a winter village. Candied ice huts polka dot the ice, trucks bumble past one another forming an ice highway. My parents slip into heavy snowsuits. They pull on insulated gloves, buckle helmets under chins, bundle the dogs into pockets on their machines or pull them behind in wide sleighs that cut into the snow, leaving snake-tailed trails behind. Great plains bellowing beneath us, little tufts of brown, skimming across the lake like angry bumble bees.

I wonder if it will swallow us, open its black mouth and tear into us, pull us into its throat, its ice bladed teeth ajar. My parents have nightmares. One morning my Ma tells us her dream with weary eyes. We are at Niagara Falls, it's winter and we get too close to these magnificent falls, the ice cracks, breaks away and we slip through, disappearing in a blink.

My Dad tucks us into a little compartment behind the snow machine. It is a homemade sleigh he has put together with some scrap wood atop blades nailed together; a little bunk for three of us and our tan dog Riley to squeeze into, covered in green vinyl. It will protect us from the biting winds that nip at our cheeks and pull us from one side of the lake, ten miles to the other. We three kids jostle side to side, huddled in the right corner, Riley on my legs. We rattle and bump. My Dad navigates his machine over the icy snow chunks until our little compartment hits an icy ridge and flips on its side; Riley's legs kick into my ribcage. We topple onto each other, the sleigh being dragged sideways, my brother and sister's weight stack upon me as we bump up and down against the snow in flashes of green vinyl. My Dad's watchful eye locates the wreck and he gallops back to us, flips open the canvas and I dash out into the vast open whiteness. Refusing to be tucked into the small rutted sleigh again, I plop my tiny body onto the long torsoed snowmachine and wrap my arms as far as I can around my Dad's waist. Shaky, I recall Riley frantically kicking me.

"How could he?" I pout to myself at the back of the roaring beast. But soon my frenzied logic flips and I wish I could pat Riley on the head and tell him we didn't mean to crash. And that sometimes, bad things happen. But only sometimes.

When dogs press against you with their long snout they usually leave a damp streak on your cheek, like a sloppy kiss. But Riley always had a terribly sensitive dry, pink nose; left in the bitter cold by his previous owners. The day we picked him up from the animal shelter, handing over one measly bill, we sat in three corners of the garage calling his name over and over, firmly believing he would come to his true owner. He drooped his back and crawled to each one of us, trembling. From that day forward we would tread our small hands into his short coat, kiss his dry nose and lay down curling up beside him wherever he was. "This dog is a real good dog" my Dad would say. He was my most loyal friend. He'd run aside our school bus on the torn back roads of Whitefish, meet us at the end of the long driveway and sit in the sandbox while we poured dirt from a bucket to bury his paws.

Winter purrs at night: a burning wood stove, crackling, icy fingers break kindling under frosty breath, steam whistles from foreheads, toques pulled tightly over ears. We scurry into the sauna as the night quietens and grows dark. We perform our sauna rituals: gathering the firewood, fetching the lake water in tall white buckets, building the fire. Patiently we wait. Some hours later one of us bundles up in the cold to stoke the fire. Embers burning within the sauna, it becomes a living entity that we tend to, care for and live in. In bathing suits or in nakedness we bellow out to the barrel shaped cedar room, barefoot or in rubber boots.

Gallant company, red faces gleaming in sweat, drinks tossed with ice cubes, old Finlanders with big bellies and naked faces bumble in. "This here is the very first barrel sauna ever built on Lake Panache," they tell us with beaming grins. They hoot and banter, pull hot salty colbassa, unwrapped from tin foil on the stove after the last cool dip in the lake. Wobbling backwards on the path, whether from a hit of steam and the icy water or from the booze, it's often hard to tell.

When you are in the sauna breathing becomes heavy. As kids we breathe through wet cloths and clamour to the bottom bench. As adults we perform *sisu,* an interior hardiness that is Finnish perseverance; else, you faint.

Cutting a hole in the ice, running the auger and long ice saw to cut a smooth shape, we purposely submerge our bodies into the icy water. Scrambling from the billowing sauna, steam a ghostly tail, we gasp as we dunk ourselves into the frigid water, surrendering as it snags our breath and sharply clasps our lungs. Bewildered, we stagger back screaming excitedly, crawling through icy patches of snow to hit a fierce wall of heat that shoots needle pricks across our skin. Our heads grow heavy and our limbs begin to tingle; the room gets hazy as though it is filled with smoke and there is this feeling that maybe we are just air.

I plunk my minnow into the ice hole and watch her swim down into the blackness, deep, deep, deeper, until I can only imagine her dashing down with the illusion of freedom, yanked back by an invisible line; a hook embodied in her shiny metallic body. I wonder if the minnow will come face to face with a toothy pike but squirm free from my J lipped hook, get away with just a war scar. Or will I feel a jagged tug, a pike having sunk its teeth into her flesh, stolen a nibble or swallowed her whole in one mighty gulp.

My Mummu sits down beside me, "Here fishy, fishy, come bite my hook," she sings gallantly. "You can be the captain and I'll be the cook!" She scoops her arm around me to squeeze, her warm, boisterous voice fills the ice hut. I wait for a playful fish wearing a sailor's hat to pop its head out of the water and sing along, "No, you can be the captain and I'll be the cook!" she'd reply.

I imagine fish below in infantry lines like soldiers, watching my minnow, jigging my line in the calculated 1-2-&-3 rhythm I see my Ma perform, impatient and yearning. I already know what will happen if I do snag one. We will all jump up in ceremonious joy, skin off her shiny armour and fry her up! Then everyone will blaze their toothy smiles over paper plates with squeezed lemons, laughing and making satisfied "mmm" noises to pick her tiny bones from our teeth.

A thin layer of ice forms atop the hole as I reel up my line. The minnow on the hook is forced to break through the smooth layer of ice with her slippery, metallic body. Her beady little black eye stares up at me. Bloodied, her chest moves up and down in panic. I flick her off the hook into the water, expecting her to dive down, but instead she floats back to the surface on her side.

One morning I awake to find Riley laying on the floor of my room in the shag rug. Shaking his yellow body to wake him up, he's cold and unmoving. I knew he had died but I wouldn't understand. Did he dissolve or float away to dog heaven, the one I knew from cartoons? Maybe he was stuck in my photographs, running in the backyard, his snout sticking out from under the bed or in the sandbox with my siblings. Every photograph I took was of Riley.

This wouldn't be the first encounter with the death of pet animals, of course. We would stumble on many of our mutts in the ditch aside the highway, just a carcass of shaggy fur, decay and bones. My sister would tear up her knees along the pavement diving down to scoop up the little bloodied body of our Dachshund, torn up by a sneering car on the wretched artery of the roads. She'd run home with the highway screaming in her ears.

Oddly enough, in the forest death was calm. It was there, but not in a frightening way. More like a pine cone dropping from a tree, the remnants of an event. The scarlet coloured carcass of a small scraggly animal, a toothy ribcage and just its tail left; like the tail shell of shrimp, the kind disposed of in the middle of shrimp trays. Long winged vultures circle, hang above the treetops, cradling shadows, stalking the grounds like a carnival swing.

Riley, who had died from a tumour, was brought to the vet for an autopsy. His organs extracted in the process, they returned him in a liquor box. My Dad, concerned, unravelled the carcass from the box and placed him on a snow float shovel covered with a sheet, so that we could have a proper burial with the remains of his body, seemingly intact. Plopping him into the divot in the hill in the marshy backyard where cattails grew, we staked a small wooden cross, nailed it together, painted it white and wrote Riley in permanent marker. I peered down into the grave before they shoveled the hill of sand, noticing that Riley's body had sunk into a few inches of murky water. I burst into tears, fumbling words about water being in his grave. How would he be okay plopped into a puddle when he was always warm-bodied and wrapped around my feet? Instead, we were dropping him into a wet hole like a minnow.

The lake rocks you at night, lulls you. The horizon expands into a vista that is the heavens: sleepy pinks and mauves swirling like cotton candy ice cream bought at the marina. The waves slow, crawling, they slosh and guzzle, curl and whoosh against the wearied rock shore. Gusts of wind growl and moan, heaving themselves; they slap the sides of the boat, throw the metal bow into the air from beneath. A storm erupts, rain slices through eavestroughs, lightning splits lanky pines into two, burning its insides. The cabin trembles in the thunder and I am reminded of our house by the railway, the relentless and steady howl of the train, its weeping lament against the track.

In the wilderness there is no danger without some uncertainty. You consider this, of course. That you could drown, your skin may sink to the bottom of the lake, you could forfeit a finger or two with the sloppy swipe of a chainsaw on a sunny day. It can become a hollow grave. In winter the lake might open up wide in the dark, crumble beneath you, its icy layers letting go. Take an arm or a leg, a fishing hole left unmasked, limbs slip down in one quick motion.

My Mummu tells us that she didn't know the lake until she lived aside it all year. In winter I've seen it open up overnight, shift in hours, moaning like thunder, become a monster pressing its arms to lift up docks, building icy pressure ridges like barricading walls or long sharp toothed trenches; a cavernous treachery. You stumble upon it like a veiled conibear trap, crooked as the ridges pressed into rock. Tragedy can murmur in the waves, appearing darker and more unforgiving than any place.

The loon throws up her wings, flailing herself at our boat that is twelve times the size of her, her white belly bellowing in and out of the water, sending a hoarse desperate scream. "We must be close to her nest," my Ma says. I am haunted by the desperation, the hostility. How animals protect their young so fiercely. Her trilling scream, so different to her ghostly howls in the stills of a summer evening.

My Mummu grabs at our hands when we visit her, her eyes well up with water, "I'm just happy," she remarks. News carries itself on the lake; warnings, good or sad tidings. A boat brings in word about a birth and that two are to be married; "so and so has had a baby, surely she will be back on the lake with her new one soon".

My Mummu's brother warns about the shifting ice. Sitting aside Mummu for coffee, she looks at us raised eyebrows using a serious tone, "if they aren't good to you," she says, referring to our partners, "well, I'll kill them. No one is not good to my grandkids," she adds.

Great Papa and Great Mummu were hunters; Great Papa trapped beaver, mink, wolves and foxes. They would hunt deer on Ella Lake or behind the farm, sleeping under the stars. Often Sylvia was the chaser, while Eino would sit atop and wait patiently for the deer. Though, one golden fall day Great Mummu would shoot and claim the largest moose of all the men in Beaver Lake.

Seasonal hunt camps left abandoned in the summer. My uncle Kevin says that my Great Mummu always loved deer fat. The year Great Mummu died he killed his biggest buck. "It must have been Mummu," he says. "It had more fat on it then any deer I've ever shot. It must have been Great Mummu's spirit helping." His eyes shine blue. Long necked tattoos down his arms, a leather skinned cowboy hat laced with teeth atop his head. He has a trapline and inherited Camp Horrible. As kids he told us stories of bears walking into his cabin when he was sleeping or floating down river on an ice chunk with his quad, attesting to strike an Elvis Presley pose if he was going to be found frozen. Uncle Kevin appreciates snowy places that have not a footprint in sight. His nickname is Bass Man along Ella Lake, but we call him our Canadian Crocodile Dundee.

Taking the familiar boat ride from the Lake Panache marina to make our voyage, I recall an old home video: my parents dancing in the kitchen in day clothes and I'm the cameraperson, sitting cross-legged, angling it towards them. The camera, unstable, sways left to right; the lens jostles towards my siblings in the living room, my parents are calling out to focus it back. It is here that I realize the trillions of moments that are always rearranging themselves, how we experience things over again, but always differently; similarities that align themselves in time. Running up a driveway that once felt miles long as thrashing rain pounds the ground, licked like a wet seal. Watching others bearing grief as time becomes opaque, an unsettling humour that becomes the face of despair. Celebrations, ceremonies and marriages where love is exchanged; where families, friends, men and women dance and drink; where women some-times change a name.

Childhood ties are sinew for remembering. They pull at you by their strings—lift you up. All of the pieces of ourselves and others become part of what we know, how we see, who we are. Familiar faces moving on the camera in saturated colours, cutting down the windbreaker tree on Christmas day, a holiday dinner at the log cabin in Beaver Lake.

Great Mummu was a Minnow Catcher, you know. The kettle screams in the kitchen. The lake takes us, breaks us and makes us.

We think about Great Mummu as she was every morning at five a.m., canoe in tow, to scoop minnows. She had a ritual, a place to wrap her hands around the paddle, a community to nestle and settle in. We do the same, in the same places. As coyotes banter in the backyard we sit around the muted fire, listen to the train rumble in the distance. Know we are home.

Always in her company. We rely on these places. Women of our own accord. I grab hold of the side of the boat as it planes out. My Ma steers the boat with ease, a small grin on her face.

We are taking the known bends, peering out towards the North Shore where the waves are rocky. On past Ben Isle, Indian Head Point, we huddle past Seagull Island, on through Burnt Island Narrows and into the bay where our humble camp awaits us; the sky and water blue as blue can be. And I remember that at the centre of my name is another, Sylvia.

Married to the lake.

Identity Confessions
By William Morin

Looking forward is blinded by peripheral distractions. Out of the corner of my eye, it's always there, residual... trauma. Along eastern shores of Lake Superior my mom's Anishinaabek / Settler mix ancestors were suffled round against their will. I inherited their geographic confusion. One generation after another, more Settler dysfunction bled the Anishinaabek from my grandparents' parents, and the rest all along the shores of Obadjiwanong (Batchawana), Goulais, Baawaating (Sault Ste. Marie), and Michipicoten.

My mom's mom, Lucy Robinson-ba, was born 1902 at the light house in Michipicoten. Her dad, Frank Gingras, was born the same year not far away, at Gros Cap, in the Northern Algoma district. The Ojibway community they were born into was relocated many times to accommodate the settler community residents; Hudson Bay trading post not wanting them too close, they were in the way of the rail line, moved to where houses were built on clay and began to sink. Today that community is now in its fifth relocation on the northern shores of Lake Superior, a twenty-minute drive on a dirt road to Wawa.

Like so many from that community who got tired of being moved around, scattered in all directions, abandoning family, land and their cultural way of life, *N'Mishoomis miinwaa Nookomis* / my grandfather and grandmother, Frank ba *miinwa* Lucy ba, relocated with some family to join some extended family south in Obadji-wanong / Batchawana Bay, a mixed blood Ojibway fishing village.

It was here they raised their family, where my *Nokomis* sold her Indian Status to an Indian Agent for $20.00 to feed her kids. It was here my *Mishoomis* taught his sons to fish, as he was taught by his ancestors. One of his sons, my mom's brother, Willy Gingras-ba, is my name sake.

This mixed blood Ojibway fishing village is where my Quebec French-speaking dad met my Ojibway-speaking mom on a blind date set up by her cousin. Mom was a single mother of two young girls and saw this union with my dad as a way out of poverty and racial oppression. Five more children came, I was the last. Sadly, two years before I was born my name sake drowned. My first few years were spent there, playing on the beach of gitchi gaamiing / the big lake, close to where Uncle Willy-ba was pulled in by the nets.

Identity hostage, royal imposition, identity ransom, genocidal decision.

My mother is Ojibway, my father was French. I am 'confusion.'
Je ne parle pas français parce que.... I do not speak my abusers' language.
N'mama Anishinaabe-kwe, niin bangii Anishinaabemowin.

Respect the Water / *Minaandendimowin Nibiish*
On the shores of Superior I entered this world.
I am a mixed child and I don't speak my native tongue.

Aaniin, Giiwedinong Enoswet Ma'iingan N'dishnikos, Baa-waa-ting miin-waa O-bad-ji-wa-nong N'donjibaa. Ma'iingan n'doodem. N'mama N'dishnikonik Bbaa-maa-she Bne-shii-nhs. N'mama Anishinaabekwe, miinwaa gashi Anishinaabemaa.

Some of my earliest memories are of swimming in Batchawana Bay. It was with my brother Marcel while our older sister, Dorothy-ba, watched from the beach. Not far, south along the shore of Lake Superior, the Edmund Fitzgerald sank. The legendary ship wreck about which Gordon Lightfoot sang, "The legend lives on from the Chippewa on down, of the big lake they call Gitche Gumee," makes me laugh cause that means 'Big Lake', on the big lake they (Ojibway / Chippewa) call 'big lake.'

Near my mother's Ojibway homeland there are ancient rock paintings.

Slowly I learn to draw spirit images and I still don't speak Ojibway.

This fluid community was now a surge in and out of our Anishinaabek cultural ways. With each ebb reflexes part of who I was, reflected back and was taken away at the same time. Ojibway identity was replaced by a settler religion, Catholic Church, and an English school that washed with alcohol all morality out of those who remained with the endless flow of vices.

Wanting the best for her children, my mother married a man who was not "native", as did her sisters. Knowing it was not going to benefit her or her children if they were "Indian" in a changing world where she had little to no control over her identity or even her ethnicity.

Dysfunctional masks paved the road into the village from the Trans-Canada Highway and tried to cover up the incest, rapes,

150 YEARS UP NORTH AND MORE

assaults and self-destruction. Auntie Anna-ba killed by a drunk driver on that road. Cousin Alfie-ba, at six years old, burnt eighty percent of his body while saving a friend from the same fate.

The first phrase I learned in Ojibwa was *shkodewaaboo naakshik minikwe,* I drink fire water in the evening.

Identity drunk, identity hangover, identity dysfunction, colonially sober.

Mom and dad had had enough and moved us to Sudbury. With hopes of better job prospects and schools for us kids, the move was not without issues. Some of the dysfunction that was all too common in the 1960s in rural Ontario followed us.

Now we were in a town with only a handful of Anishinaabek / mixed blood families; we stood out. Going to and from school daily had its challenges. Like a target everyday each of us maneuvered the school yard mind / mine fields. Bullies calling us out on the bus and in the schools, "skwaas," "wagon burners," "Indian givers" and other slurs of hate and ignorance.

It was too late for my older siblings to shake off the dirt of shame which drove them down paths of self-destruction. Due to the short exposure in that mixed blood mixed up blur of colonial collisions, as the youngest, I was spared, some......what. However, this reality hovers over me like an umbrella of axes, never knowing when, or if it will fall /fail.

Dysfunction road / rode like a rez dog, it was always nipping at my heals / heels, and no way to tame it. Out of the corner of my eye, traumas wormed their way into full view. Abuse came in waves when family back home would come to visit. Seeing it as normal made it easy for me to dismiss it, and occupy myself with my love of art and the natural world.

96

The more I discover our shared history the more I search the water, *ndawaabdan nibiing.*

In school, in the playground I was the Indian kid, until they learned my father was French, then..... "So you're mixed, you must be Metis."

Identity theft, identity delusion, identity assumption, identity confusion.

But, was I Metis? If I was, what about my Ojibway grandparents, don't they count or only the French count? Do I choose, or is the choice made for me? Does my mom's ancestry disappear because I am mixed, even if she still speaks an Indigenous language that is older than Europe?

It was through my artistic journey that I gained identity clarity, which guided me to harvesting the fruits of blood memory.

Along the shore I paddle my canoe with the dancing waves, *Jiigabiing n'jiimed n'jiimaaning niime niibi.*

The issue of mixed racial identity in Canada began nine months after the first settlers / colonizers arrived. The children of mixed unions were instrumental in the building of what is Canada today.

Eventually when enough of them were born and their blood was shed in defense of their families, on a land in a specific western geography, where they merged languages over time in history, they earned the right to call their own, to call themselves the Metis, the historical Metis.

This ongoing confusion is complicated on a number of the loose and arbitrary governmental or personal categorical determinants leading many over generations to self-identify as Métis based on

150 YEARS UP NORTH AND MORE

these settler safe determinants. This is compounded by the educational, public and historical assumptions of a simplification to cultural identity, of what is a métis, not who are the Métis. I was told I was Métis, I was not asked.

Weaving images of spirit animals and giant serpents across time on the walls of Agawa, Mishibizhii, the Great Lynx painted red, a prehistoric fresh water dragon, stands watch.

I am mixed but I am not métis / Métis, I am an aapita Anishinaabe nini / a mixed Ojibwa man. That is when I began my reclamation, rebuilding my identity. This too was not without individual and community identity wars with governmental policies in the Indian Act still in place today.

One of the few changes, Bill C-31, an Act to Amend the Indian Act, in 1985, was the first of two more to come in small attempts to remove the sexual discrimination in the Indian Act. Women who lost their status were now able to regain it, giving them the right to pass it on to their children. That is what my mom did.

Indigenous ethnic battle fields where brother would fight brother as to who was more "Indian", who was more traditional, who had more rights than another, who looked more "Indian", status, non status, Bill C-31 and enfranchised. Whatever it was, we all were wounded, where wounded Indians would wound Indians, adding to the layers of lead paint of intergenerational trauma.

Semaa nbagidinaa nibiing, Tobacco I offer to the water, for safe passage on *zaaghigan / Gichi-gamii,* the big lake.

The summer of 1990, I was serving as a Medical Assistant, posted to Cornwallis, Nova Scotia. That same summer, the Oka Crisis

98

broke out, then the first Gulf War. The layers of colonial / Settler ignorance began to chip away. That same October I received a letter from the Department of Indian Affairs and under Bill C-31; I was granted Indian Status. My mom, seen as a White woman for sixty years by the government and then, like magic, poof, she is deemed an Indian, even though she speaks Ojibwa as did her parents, and their parents...in the land of their Anishinaabek ancestors.

Colonization had one goal: a historical erasure of tribal peoples and their tribal names from the land Settlers wanted. Systemic public shaming and labeling lead many of our people to paint themselves with the wide white brush of assimilation.

The inter-generational identity trauma lead many mixed blood Indigenous peoples into cutting denial along cultural wrists to cut off branches of our family trees, ethnic pruning / self-inflicted identity crimes, to hide their "indianness" as a form of survival in an imposing colonial Canada. It was safer to say you were French or English.

Ginaabik biishoo, ganawaamjiged gimishkwaabik moona'igan zaaghigan.

The serpent like bobcat guards the ancient copper mines of these lakes.

Almost forty years ago, the fall of 1979, my sister Dorothy baa died at seventeen years of age, collateral damage of Settler arrogance. She was beginning to heal; returning home early from a party, she was hit by one of two cars drag racing, a few blocks from our house. The young man driving the car that hit her received three weekends in jail as punishment. He was a university student.

Just recently, Brock Turner sexually assaulted Susan Miller while she was unconscious. The assailant was sentenced to six months in county jail, released after three months. The victim, Susan Miller,

150 YEARS UP NORTH AND MORE

was celebrated as 2016 Woman of the Year by Glamour Magazine. For decades, thousands of Indigenous women in Canada, North America, go missing or are murdered. They are not acknowledged. The launch of the National Inquiry of Missing and Murdered Indigenous Women has given voice to families of those women and their pain. Indigenous people do not have a history, they have a now. What has happened, is happening, and will continue to happen until we all change.

Twenty years after my sister passed I returned to the same university the young man who killed her attended, where I now teach Indigenous Studies, helping to continue her healing, our healing. It appears after two decades of teaching I began to understand my mom's path to survival. This helped me to see more and more why people of mixed ancestry hid their "indianness", and how some still do. Slowly I see younger people feeling safer to come forward, halfway, to publicly acknowledge their past.

Recognizing intergenerational identity confusion, I witness some of these students in their struggles through their parents' identity wounds from colonial crimes and settler self- preservation, where family were lost among the red wood and the white birch in their forest of ancestors.

In the age of the Royal Commission on Aboriginal Peoples (RCAP) and the United Nations Declaration on the Rights of Indigenous Peoples, it is safer and sexier now to be "Indian" or Indigenous.

Gawii ndoo oonenzen semaa wii bagidinag minaandemaa nibi, Mishipizhoo giishpin comaajiidik naamii'ying nibiing.

I cannot tell you who you are, but I will ask, who are your ancestors? It is part of Anishinaabek introductions, Mino bimaadiziwin / Ojibway way of the good life is to introduce who we are, where

100

we are from and what is our spirit name. This is so that we may find connections in others; to family, to a place, or on a spiritual level.

More importantly, we do not need to hide behind a term (Métis) that only adds to the colonial goal to erase Indigenous peoples / tribes by name. Those of us who are of Indigenous ancestry, we can honour your Indigenous ancestors. When we honour them, it is important to also honour our Anishinaabek teachings, to honour the four directions, and all our ancestors equally.

Aaniin Gchi-Manidoo, Mishomisak, miinwaa N'ookimisak.

Giiwedinong Eniwed Ma'iingan N'dishnikos, Ma'iingan n'doodem. Baawaating miinwaa Obadjiwanong N'donjibaa. N'mama zhinikaaso Beatrice Gingras.

Miigwetch.

The Original Hard Woman
By Shawna Diane Partridge

Like most of her stories, this one is no different, prefaced with instructions: "Now don't tell anyone!"

Mother yells over the phone partially from excitement, mostly because our family is comprised of loud women. "Want to hear a good story?" she asks me.

"Sure, but I'm at work. Can't really talk now."

"Just listen then—Now don't tell anyone..."

"Who am I going to tell?"

"Your sister, I don't know, anyone. Are you going to listen or not?" The gossip commences. "Well..."

The story, so detailed, seems almost shocking. My tight-lipped family would not approve.

I hear a smile in Mother's voice. "That's what I said. Then the store owner was like, 'What?'"

Mother walks into a small antique store on John Street. It connects to Northland Road where she grew up and my grandparents still reside. She's lived here her entire life in Sault Ste. Marie, Ontario.

No larger than our kitchen, the store still manages to house more collectibles than my mother's and grandmother's homes combined. Antiques stacked onto more antiques, floor to ceiling, crowding every inch of that store. Mother can barely make out one item from the plenty, her eyes unable to rest. Antiques, now worthless from the way they've been displayed.

Mother came to search and pass the time, mining for buried treasures: chipped cups, collectible cameras, my inheritance. She digs, scans, rummages through, trying to see all that the store has to offer. Behind the pillars of merchandise, paintings, photographs, and plates line the walls. As high as the ceiling, they hang. No space left unclaimed.

She faces the store owner who eagerly stands behind the cash register. Finding nothing she likes, Mother thanks the owner for her time. There's too much to see and buy. She fears disturbing the delicate balance of the piles. One item removed and it might come tumbling down, the entire store, building and all.

She turns to leave, nodding to the owner who nods back as if to reply, "maybe next time." Mother wavers a moment, feeling compelled to stop. She glances towards the ceiling and squints. A portrait. A family. Her family.

She takes a step toward the cash. "What are you doing with my grandmother?"

It all started with Great-Grandmother. A line of hard women descended.

Growing up, there were no framed photos of Great-Grandmother in our house, none in Grandmother's either. Family photos weren't on display for guests to see, not even of me or my sister. We did have stacks of albums bursting with photos, tucked away in closets collecting souvenirs of age. More dust. My family quietly loved.

Great-Grandmother Yawdokia had thick hands indicative of her personage and personality. Although I had only seen her in photographs, I could tell she had the hands of a worker. Those hands embodied everything that a hard woman is. They were rough, calloused, engraved with palm lines from being worn in like leather gloves. I imagined her rubbing them constantly but never complaining of the pain. Strong but nimble hands, able to knead dough effortlessly and delicate enough to shape *pedaha* into perfect-sized dumplings. Hands that disciplined her children, rarely used in a reassuring caress. An unconventional woman in a time of men.

I knew her.

I took her to be a quiet woman with a great voice. Spoke up when required, she laid down the law and then returned to her silent authority. Respected when quiet, even more so when she had something to say. Hardly a tranquil or calm woman, not that type of quiet. Not a soft woman. It was just that she didn't have to speak to be heard. Her presence alone commanded respect. A force to be reckoned with. Ruthless, determined; a survivor. No, a trailblazer.

I knew her.

This is who I have to live up to. This woman, I looked for.

Great-Grandmother died in August of 1988. Placed in the local newspaper Sault Star, a "CARD OF THANKS":

The family of the late Yawdokia wish to express their heartfelt appreciation and thanks to relatives and friends for their many thoughts of kindness, messages of sympathy, visits to the funeral home, contributions of time, food, flowers, donations and cards during the recent loss of our dear mother and grandmother. [...] Our mother and grandmother will be fondly remembered by all.

Besides when custom dictated, my family rarely spoke of Great-Grandmother after her death. They didn't speak of the past. It just wasn't done. I felt destined to know her though. I would become determined to, desperately pulling on this string of the past to see it clearer.

Born in November of 1988, I resembled the maternal side of my family: dark, loud, with Ukrainian tan skin. Carved in newspaper ink, the horoscope on my birthdate predicted:

SCORPIO [Oct. 23-Nov. 21]
Be aware of polls, statistics, personal potential. Check meanings, implications, subtle clues. Family member wants to tell you something but is hesitant. Be analytical, show willingness to communicate.

What did she want to tell me? Why hesitant? It didn't seem in her nature.

I needed to know more. The secrecy made our family history all the more attractive. As a child and adolescent, I would sneak eavesdropping on Mother and Grandmother. I would overhear fragments, morsels like: "a strong lady"; "good woman"; had nine children, you know?" When caught and Mother thought I heard too much, I would be instructed, "Now don't tell anyone!"

Confused, I questioned: "Tell, who? Tell, what? I don't know anything. If they can talk about it, why can't I? What's the big deal?"

I didn't understand, no, but I listened, yes. Mother told me not to. I shared what little I knew with no one: friends, sister, nobody. Mother must have had her reasons, though none were provided. Besides, she was my mother and a hard woman herself, one you listened to. I maintained our secrecy, our custom of silence, but I continued to gather more secrets. Mother said nothing about that, only that we mustn't share.

Mother walks into that antique store, not searching for anything in particular. She is "just looking", although she takes this looking business very seriously, just as I took my search for Great-Grandmother when it became a full-time preoccupation.

It was two years before the discovery of our family portrait, that I first found Great-Grandmother for myself. Living in Windsor, Ontario, I amassed a small group of close friends, all fellow writers. At that time, I was pencilling stories about this-and-that, nothing worth reading, so I decided to write one about my family. Just one. What did I have to lose? No one knew my family. The physical distance from Sault Ste. Marie gave me leeway to disconnect emotionally, or at least that was what I thought. My first story focusing on my heritage went over well with my writer friends. The story had depth. I thought to write more stories about my relatives but even with the geographical distance, I couldn't. I remembered my mother's words, repeated throughout my childhood, "Now don't tell anyone!" I chose not to write about them anymore, loosely or otherwise. I was taught better.

Buried in lifeless writing, I persisted in creating worlds, extravagant characters, and wordy descriptions. Nothing relatable. No universal feelings or human nature portrayed. It was more important to write about anything but my family than concentrate on what I was actually creating.

Great-Grandmother was interesting. The same thoughts occupied my mind for months but remained unanswered: "Why couldn't I write about her? One more story and only about her."

I re-replayed the same memory from my childhood, another of Mother's lessons.

"Why don't we talk about Great-Grandmother?" From the secrets I had compiled quietly over the years, I knew she had did something wrong, something illegal.

"We just don't talk about it," was Mother's explanation.

"But why?"

"We just don't, that's why," she paused. "It just doesn't make us look good."

"What doesn't? To who?"

"It just doesn't."

"But why?" could be the title of my childhood. I needed to understand why my family was who they were.

In my one-bedroom apartment in Windsor, I would sit at my writing desk waiting for inspiration to rush over me. It never came. Again and again, I returned to the idea of my family wondering how could I write a story about Great-Grandmother without mentioning her children, the house they grew up in, her past, her future, our family. That way, only the dead were discussed. Again and again, I remembered, "We just don't talk about it." The past was too far gone, not to be disturbed by the present.

Our past: who we were and are, had to be preserved. More questions arose: "After Grandmother passes away? Mother? Who will remember? Will we have only fragments of fragments?"

I don't remember when I decided to write about them. But I did. I was going to talk about my family. In order to do so, however, I felt compelled to lie. Scared of my family's reactions, I revealed little of my true intentions to them.

Several times, I travelled home to Sault Ste. Marie to sift through the local archives. I dug through dusty paper, scrolled through microfilm of old newspaper, read local history books, and listened to recorded oral histories.

Searching through historical databases, I located dates, numbers, facts. I found my great-grandparents' marriage license.

Yawdokia immigrated to Canada in what must've been the late 1920s, as she was married shortly thereafter in Sault Ste. Marie in 1932. Young Yawdokia wedded fellow Ukrainian Immigrant, Nicholas. He was 27; she was 18. They carved out their life in Northern Ontario where her children and onwards would furrow deeper roots.

The certificate identifies them as Catholics. In looping cursive,

107

150 YEARS UP NORTH AND MORE

the Priest spelt her name as "Eudokia." My family assures me it's spelt "Yawdokia" in English. The translation is never perfect.

Both Yawdokia and Nicholas could read and write in English though. As the certificate states:

Can bridegroom read? Yes write Yes

Can bride read? Yes write? Yes

It was *in the Country of Algoma this ninth day of July 1932,* my great-grandparents married, and our family of hard women in Canada began.

What I couldn't find in recorded history, I sought in cups of tea and conversation.

Accompanied by Mother, I visited Grandmother's oldest sister for the first time. One of her sisters-in-law was also visiting. I didn't question why Mother decided to come with me. It was nice to having three generations sitting around one table enjoying tea and cookies.

My great-aunts seemed happy to talk about their childhoods. Their excitement was sadly shadowed by unease. I was stunned by their uncharacteristic openness compared to my immediate family. They were different, but why? I'm still trying to figure this out.

While my great-aunts were so open, I was not. I wished to learn about their lives and by extension, Great-Grandmother for what I explained as a school project, not a novella I hoped one day would be published into a book for all to read. They shared stories and sips of tea. I shared little of my intentions. I thought, learned, it was best not to share all.

Mouth full of cake, I asked, "Tell me...what...what was Great-Grandmother like? What was it like growing up in the Sault of your era? 1940s? 50s?"

My grandmother's oldest sister, then in her late eighties, narrated her life growing up in a three-storey boarding house on Queen Street West, owned and operated by my great-grandparents.

108

Eight rooms on the top floor were rented out to boarders. Tall and thin, the boarding house also fit a pool hall and neighbourhood bar within its walls. It seems Great-Grandmother Yawdokia, never called by her first name by patrons, ran the makeshift bar during the Prohibition until the early 1960s. She sold watered-downed whiskey from bottles filled with pour-backs. Shots were 25 cents, and never went to waste.

Selling alcohol illegally did come at a price. Great-Grandmother was arrested several times for her illegal business. Thinking it indecent to jail a woman, wife, and mother, police refused to arrest her. They insisted on arresting her husband. Far from a conventional woman, Great-Grandmother forced the police to lock her up for her own crimes, not her husband. If he missed work, Great-Grandfather might have lost his job. Even with all the side businesses, money was tight for this family of eleven during The Depression.

If she was arrested, surely, there would be record of it in the newspapers. I searched, gauging the period of the arrests. My great-aunts couldn't remember exact dates. They were too old then.

On microfilm preserved newspapers, records of men arrested for similar crimes. I couldn't find accounts of women being arrested reported in the newspapers. It happened; Great-Grandmother was proof of that.

I was going to be like her, fearless, so I visited Grandmother to ask about her mother. My own mother came with me. Her opinion changing after hearing our family's stories. With her by my side, I walked through my grandmother's front door.

Mother said bluntly to Grandmother, "She's hear to ask you questions," pointing to me.

I turned on the tape recorder in my pocket. I didn't inform Grandmother that I was recording our conversation. I felt guilty, but that was my chance to hear our stories. I had waited years to hear her talk about the past, not in passing or through whispers, but openly and to me. I ensured I'd remember exactly what she said.

My guilt, however, did carry with me for the next few days. I had the answers that I desired for so long. The stories were there on my tape recorder and building in my imagination. I wished to listen to the recording to replay Grandmother's words, but I was still too ashamed of my actions and secrecy.

After a few days, I chose to transcribe the conversation to have Great-Grandmother's life finally in ink and recorded. This hard woman existed.

Date of Interview: 29 November 2014
Time: 5:45 p.m.
Duration: approx. 30 minutes
Place: Sault Ste. Marie, Ontario
Interviewer: Shawna Partridge
Participant: Grandmother (age 83)

I: What was it like growing up in a boarding house with bootlegging going on? What was it like?

P: What was it like? It was work. We had to clean all the rooms upstairs. We were little. My mother was strict. We cleaned all the rooms. Then we had bootlegging.

I: How old were you?

P: Oh, we were young. Like in that casket photograph of my brother Adolf, when he passed away.

I: So you must've been like sixish?

P: Oh yeah. And we had to go upstairs and clean all the rooms.

I: You were cleaning at six years old?

P: Yeah. Oh yeah.

I: What was your mother like?

P: My mother was a good woman. Yeah—

I: Yeah?

P: Yeah. She was good. She stayed home. She was like, like I say,

SHAWNA DIANE PARTRIDGE

she got mad at times but when you got eight kids, and my dad used to drink, ya know, too. So yeah—so how's everything down there in Windsor?

I: I really wanted to come home. I really wanted to come home.

P: You had to get away?

I: I had to get away. I like living in Windsor, but ya know—

P: So what other questions you got?

I: Your mother... got arrested a couple of times, didn't she?

P: Yeah.

I: When it happened, how old were you?

P: We were young. We were young 'cause my dad said he used to... feed us sour milk in a baby bottle. He couldn't take care of us. [laughing] I don't know how come they put her in jail. Well, she was caught bootlegging.

I: So what was the charge? Bootlegging?

P: Yeah.

I: How long was she in jail for? Like how many days?

P: Maybe say—now that I wouldn't know. It wasn't that long. They wouldn't keep her that long. No. No. Maybe a couple of days.

I: Did they charge her? Did she have to pay money?

P: She probably had to pay a fine, yeah. I still remember upstairs—we slept upstairs, and the police used to come upstairs. Search it.

I: Really? In your little apartment in the boarding house?

P: Oh yeah! That was bootlegging. Like ya know, Al Capone days, ya know? [laughing] Oh yeah. With flashlights, I remember the police shining it in our faces eh. We were little.

I: How many years did your mother do bootlegging for?

P: My mother? Oh, she did it for a long time. Till... she moved to the other house—the one on Queen Street that was the one she did the bootlegging in.

I: Yeah. The boarding house?

P: Yeah.

111

I: They tore it down, right?
P: Oh it's all gone. The bridge took everything.

Great-Grandmother's three-storey boarding house and everything it contained were torn down in the early 1960s. It had to be demolished to make way for the International Bridge that would connect Sault Ste. Marie, Ontario to Sault Ste. Marie, Michigan. Where that boarding house once stood, now stands a pier for the bridge, supporting it, bearing its weight.

The bridge didn't take everything as Grandmother had said. Great-Grandmother was there as she always had been, a pillar of familial and female strength.

Mother walked into that small antique store on John Street looking for nothing in particular. John connecting to Northland Road and her childhood home, and running into Queen Street West where Yawdokia's pillar stands. Mother discovered something worth having: a portrait of Great-Grandmother and her family in Ukraine.

It's a black-and-white photograph cased in an ebony frame with yellowed convex glass. The photo captures five slightly smiling faces: in the centre, Great-Grandmother's father, then her brother and sister, and her sister's husband, and in the top right, Yawdokia.

Mother says the store owner seemed embarrassed, thinking that the owner had purchased the photograph along with other antiques from a couple who had visited the store looking to sell. The owner had a feeling she shouldn't have bought the items; something hadn't seemed right. But there Great-Grandmother was for purchase.

Before calling me, Mother had called Grandmother. She, too, had heard the story. Grandmother, too, had been instructed to tell no one. Mother would eventually show her the photo, and Grandmother would identify her mother and extended family in it.

Mother would also learn that the photo had belonged to one

of my great-aunts. Burglarized, Great-Aunt's house had been ransacked. It seems our family heirlooms had been peddled to antique stores, pawn shops, yard sales.

The owner had priced our family portrait at $50. Mother bartered, paid $40 for it, and took Great-Grandmother home. Mother found something out of the plenty, after all.

The family portrait had travelled great distances, somehow finding its way from Ukraine to Sault Ste. Marie, to one of my great-aunt's houses, stolen and then illegally sold to an antique store, and finally landing in Mother's possession.

My journey to find Yawdokia and accept my family seemed just as long. Living in Windsor, miles from Sault Ste. Marie, I told Great-Grandmother's story and my own. I wrote a fiction to fill in gaps that no memory and no history book could fill. Fiction to honour my family and respect them. Often too secretive, my family, but nonetheless, their ways deserving of respect.

Great-Grandmother's determined spirit infused my writing. Her extraordinary life shared because women like her did and do live. Because the colourful stories are not recorded in history books. Because, I found her and myself in my writing about the past and my family.

Some of my family members have read my novella, now published. They've attended my readings of the book. I think they're proud of our history and me.

Until now, Great-Grandmother and the family portrait had been hidden away in Mother's basement. It had been stored like all our family photographs, old and current.

It's time they were displayed. Journeying from Ukraine and the far past, the family portrait deserves to be hung and celebrated. Because our family speaks about the past, now.

And there she is. And there I am. Hard women to find. Hard women in life.

A Farewell To Steam
By Rod Carley

Boxcar row, North Bay, Ontario, 1957.

The transient camp of railway men and their families, immigrants, hobos and stray dogs for nearly thirty years. All coming and going from North Bay during the age of steam.

North Bay was the hub of Northern Ontario railroading and the adopted home for many living out their days, young and old alike, in converted boxcars moored on a railway siding about five miles outside of town.

They called this place, *Train Town,* and these are some of their stories and tall tales—captured with the colour and spirit of their own voices.

The Track Was Not Level

They had a guy called a tie-spotter, and what he did, was he went along, he had a paintbrush on a stick, and he actually walked the rails. And he would dab the ties that need replacing. So, he was actually walking...

So then, after he had put all those spots, he would add them up—let's say there were a thousand—then they would load a thousand ties, on a, what they call a work-train. And the work-train would come along at a very slow pace...and the guy would walk beside the work-train—there'd be workers up on the train—and every time he saw one of those spots they'd throw a tie off.

Throw a tie off.

Throw a tie off.

So all these ties would be lying along the side of the rail bed, for twenty miles....

Then we would come, the extra gang, and we would see all these spots...so, you'd...jack the rails up, pull the old ties out, put the new ties in, and pack all the ballast up, and do all these other things –

I can remember...like it was yesterday, Andy Sauzeville. He was the section man, eh? A big Czech. He was our boss and he was standing there, keep in mind, like this is in the middle of the summer, it's hot. And you're shoveling ballast, and I can remember Andy standing there and saying...

"I don't know what I'm going to do, uh, you guys are not near as good as the bunch I had last year, because the bunch I had last year, they could replace 160 to 170 ties a day, day in and day out. In fact, there was one day that they replaced 185 ties!"

Well, that's all we needed to hear. We would work like dogs to replace 185 ties. Damn true!

Raise A Glass

Some say that William Van Horne, the CPR's first president, ran the railways with an iron fist. Likely they were victims of his strict liquor policies. Now Van Horne could not bear the sight of a drunk. Upon learning the CPR trains sold whiskey in the dining cars he immediately banned the practice, stating it was below the

150 YEARS UP NORTH AND MORE

railway's dignity.

After a while the rules changed a little. It was now okay to drink if you bought your booze at the company bar, but it was still a loathsome offense, worthy of arrest, if you cracked open a bottle you brought on yourself. Like all rules, these restrictions inspired defiant deeds. When railway employees weren't looking, you'd see flasks and bottles appear from the most unlikely hiding places: knitting bags, kids' lunch pails and hatboxes. Once, I even saw an Irish priest step into the vestibule and whip out a bottle from under his clerical robe.

Police raids turned up caches of illegal liquor in freight-car animal carcasses and baggage-car trunks crammed with hollowed-out books. Whether in the bar car or on their own, some passengers could not imagine taking a northern journey without paying throat service to the "demon brew."

The Christmas Raffle

The Christmas raffle. Boy, oh boy. That was a time.

I immigrated to Canada from Galway in 1921. After gettin' laid off from me weldin' job at Massey-Harris, I got a job as a newsie on the trains. Well, it wasn't long after starting to work on the trains when I figured out to make some extra money—bootleggin'. My friends would buy me mickeys for $2.35 and I would sell them to passengers for $5.00. I'm on the Toronto-North Bay run, and it's Christmas Eve, and we're making our way up to North Bay. I'm making a killin'. Over six hundred bucks worth of liquor sold. Every mickey gone except one. So many people asked for it that I suggested a raffle. Twelve tickets for $2.00 apiece. One guy buying a raffle ticket was really obnoxious. He was so drunk that he could hardly stand up and yet he insisted that he needed another drink. His wife was fed up. Fuming mad. She said repeatedly that she'd had enough and he'd answer her back with lines like: "Shut up or I'll shut you up."

Guess who won the draw? Of course, it was the obnoxious creep. Now his wife was somethin' else. She was French Canadian, twelve years older than me, and not a bad looker. She asked me if she could accompany me to the baggage car to claim her husband's prize. Now the baggage car is where the *newsies* kept these large steamer trunks filled with ice to keep the pop cold. It's also where we stashed the booze. The *newsies* were the only ones who had the keys.

That's also where they kept the mailbags. Once we got to the baggage car, she said her husband was a pain and a half and she wished she was traveling with a nice young lad like me. Well, I'm no Albert Einstein but I knew what she was drivin' at. We started neckin' and then we settled down to... play some checkers.

When we were finished, I unlocked the trunk and gave her the mickey. We went back to the coach, and her husband had passed out. She looked at her husband and then she looked at me and whispered into my ear, "Good night."

I never saw her again. The woman and her husband got off the train an hour later but let me tell you, I had a smile on my face all the way to New Year's Eve.

Proud Canadian

Swanson's horn was the undoing of a moose. Swanson was the Vancouver inventor who created an ingenious horn for a cross-Canada train tour. The national train tour commission thought it was marvelous. The engineer pulled a cord and the horn played the opening notes of "O Canada."

The Department of Transport didn't share our view. It said the horn confused railyard workers and might cause an accident. So it banned the horn in cities and at level crossings. The bad news for the moose was that it could still be used in the uninhabited wild.

Some guy at the controls somewhere along the dark forests of Northern Ontario rounded a bend and saw this magnificent Bull Moose in the centre of the tracks. He couldn't stop in time. He yanked the cord and "O Canada" resounded off the Canadian Shield. The moose was a true Canadian. He didn't run. He snapped smartly to attention, his head up, his eyes glowing with nationalistic fervor. They say he died instantly.

Worth Waiting For

Cafes near the train stations had their specialties: maybe it's their breakfast, maybe roast beef. If you boarded a train with no diner in the 1940's, better hope for a *l-o-n-g* stop near a good cafe. In North Bay: Mrs. Demarco and her raisin pie!

Joan Vendetti arrived in North Bay in 1929 from Frosolone, Italy, at the age of nine. She became the beloved baking wife of Tony Demarco.

The Cochrane train would stop in town and folks would rush to Demarco's for slices of pie. One time about twenty people trooped into the café and Mrs. Demarco ran out of raisin pie.

The conductor said, "I want some so bad I'll wait till a new batch comes out of the oven."

"What about our schedule?" asked the train's Engineer.

"You don't have to worry. We'll make it to Cochrane okay," said the conductor.

The train was late getting away, but it was in on the dot in Cochrane. How come?

She bore down the track like a crazy demon—cars swayed so bad, the passengers banged into walls; a pregnant lady said it was liable to bring her baby before its time!

The cafes near the railways were better. ....McDonald's? ...
Kentucky Fried? –that's like comparing donkeys to thoroughbreds.

The Great Depression

When the stock market plunged in 1929, the Golden Age of
Northern Ontario railroading was abruptly terminated. Locomo-
tives began hauling lines of empty boxcars, and the passengers were
largely of the non-paying variety; freight-hopping hobos raking the
land in search of work.

My uncle, a silver miner in Cobalt, became one of those hobos.
He'd arrived in Northern Ontario from Birmingham shortly after
the *Titanic* sunk.

"Riding the rods sure rattled your bones," he'd say. "You'd be
down 'neath a boxcar, hanging on for dear life, while the train acted
like she wanted to throw you off."

Now, the rod-riders weren't rough guys. The odd one was but
most were nice, ordinary fellows. In the Depression, men helped
each other. They'd tell you where the best soup kitchens were or
who might have a bit of work for you. The Catholic priests were
great. Go to church and you'd be sure of some bread and a piece of
cheese.

The women? Nobody laid a finger on them. There were a few
winos or whores, but most were on the trains because they were
hoping a new city meant new luck.

The Two Commandments

Vic and I rode the freights from Timmins to Vancouver. Vic's
my brother. He was the mayor of Hamilton for fourteen years. Our
folks came to Timmins from Poland before Vic and I were born.
In 1936 we were restless kids who wanted to see the country. We

went into the jungle and the hobos made sure we didn't starve. We stoked hay for money and did temporary factory jobs. The emphasis should be on the word "temporary." A boss would pick Vic and me out of a crowd and hire us because he could pay kids fifty cents less than he paid adults. At noon, he'd go back to the crowd at the gate and say, "Any of you fellas willing to work for a boy's wages?" Two guys would say yes and he'd sack us on the spot.

There were two Commandments I heard many times on the road: "Thou shalt not mess with Capreol Red" and "Thou shalt not go into Sudbury."

Sudbury had a reputation of being a company town and that company was the CPR. If a hobo was caught by the Mounties on the streets of Sudbury he was nailed for trespassing on CPR property and jailed for thirty days. You had to leave the freight after the tunnel and walk miles through the bush to catch another train on the far side of town.

Capreol Red was a sweetheart. They don't make them like that anymore, thank goodness. He acquired his nickname because he had this thick Irish red hair and he patrolled the railyards at Capreol. The rail-riders hated him. If he nabbed you on a freight, he'd belt you with a two-by-four.

They used to have iceboxes in some of the old boxcars to keep fruit and things in. These iceboxes had clasp-locks on them. The story goes that a band of hobos lay in wait for Capreol Red and stuffed him in an icebox. He was found dead weeks later.

What's the name of that TV show? "Believe It Or Not?" I'm inclined to believe it. He had enough enemies.

Silas Huntington

Oh! And Yeah! Boxcars performed another first:
Sure they carried freight, but they served to quench a

spiritual thirst!
As is often the case, in our immigrant frontier,
Came the Methodist cause, to allay our fears.
Silas Huntington!
He came in 1880 up the Ottawa,
Followed the voyageurs along the Mattawa;
Strong in physique as well as belief—
At fifty years of age he could lift a side of beef.
Huntington!
...with one hand.
Silas Huntington!
He comforted the poor, and he preached wide and far
From his favourite place of worship – CPR boxcars.
His faith in God was indestructible!
And his faith in Man as intractable –
When he knelt on an out crop of Ancient Shield,
The future of the North was to him revealed:
"One day, this country will be people with farms and factories,
with towns and cities...!"
Silas,
Huntington!

Boxcar Schoolhouse

You met the greatest people on the railroad. People you planned to meet again so you could repay their kindness but you never did. Like the Slomans, Fred and Cela. From Clinton. They were the very first to run a railway school in Canada. Pioneers. They started in the 1920s and all through the Depression they stayed at it.

Out in the wilds, where there were no regular schools, just fur trappers, loggers, families of section men.

What the Slomans did was take their schoolhouse, an old CPR

121

150 YEARS UP NORTH AND MORE

boxcar, from town to town in Northern Ontario. The Slomans didn't turn up their noses at anybody. Not even a filthy bum like I was in them days.

The school part of the boxcar had a stove, a pull-down map of the world—and the sun never set on the pink British Empires—wooden desks in a row and the Union Jack.

On the floor of the boxcar, there was a big old car battery. The Slomans used it to operate a beat-up projector and show educational movies about beavers and birds. Not just to kids—their friends and families as well.

Night classes with kerosene lanterns blazing in the winter. The Slomans would teach the grown-ups to r-e-a-d and w-r-i-t-e.

The part of the car the Slomans lived in was small. But it was clean and done-up okay: lace curtains, flowers in clay pots, a big bearskin rug on the floor.

I was walking on the tracks at Temagami in '34, and their boxcar was on a siding. The missus was standing beside it, washing clothes in a copper tub. She asked where I was off to and I said Toronto. Her husband poked his head out the door and said, "Why don't you stay for lunch?"

I hadn't eaten for a while; I was in no position to say no.

On school days, kids would come all over the map anyway they could. All nationalities. In the winter, they'd walk miles on snowshoes; the summers they paddled canoes or hitched rides in hand cars.

One Greek mother brought her three kiddies six miles on foot to be in class. The four of them sat at the back, asking questions once in a while. At three, they left.

As they got to the door, the mother turned to Fred Sloman and said, "My kids were nagging me to give them an education. I'm glad they finally got one. Thank you very much."

122

The family tramped off into the bush and never came back.

Military Train

In 1942, the Canadian Government sent a special train across the country. Everybody was talking about it. Me and some buddies trudged down to North Bay to look it over. Tanks and jeeps and howitzers and Lews machine-guns on the flat cars. Spellbinding stuff for us teenagers. They had steps you went up and you could touch the guns and imagine what it was like to shoot them.

Inside the coaches, it was another story. Uniforms draped on department-store dummies, and pistols, medals, pictures of soldiers training displayed in glass cases. On the walls there were pictures of the King and Queen and Prime Minister Mackenzie King. Jeepers, what a show. All intended to glorify war and make you want to sign up right away.

It was typical of us Canadians that they didn't have recruitment people on the train, and no band playing "O Canada." The Americans would've had a band blasting "The Battle Hymn of the Republic," a brigade of soldiers shoving pens under everybody's noses and maybe a picture of Hitler with a target painted on his chest. But us kids got the message.

We couldn't wait to be old enough to join up. We were bear cubs and the military train was the honey that lured us.

Fearless Frank

We knew this guy called Fearless Frank, after a character in the Dick Tracy comic strip. He was this German with an ugly scar. He wasn't exactly a hero to the youngsters in my neighbourhood but we did make admiring jokes about his peculiar passion. Around 1950, Fearless Frank was arrested in Kapuskasing for trying to steal a locomotive. It was revealed in court that he'd committed the same offence before in other Canadian cities. Wearing a railway uniform, he'd climb into the cab of an unattended locomotive and head for the main line, defying the potential danger posed by oncoming trains.

Wake-Up Call

I was fifteen when I got out of Ireland, and soaking wet behind the ears when it came to dealing with adults. I had signed on with the railroad in North Bay as a callboy. Not everybody in town had a phone and what the callboy did was go around to a railwayman's house and tell him when he had to report for a shift. Most of the time you'd be dragging some guy out of bed at three in the morning so he'd be ready for a 12-hour shift.

Henry Mummery scared me. He weighed three hundred pounds. He played professional football in America before the railway. I recollect going to his place at 5:00 a.m. and he was already up, at the kitchen table, looking into space.

"They want you for the 6:30 run, Mr. Mummery."

"Do they now? Well, maybe Sunny Jim, I don't want them."

I didn't argue. I got out as fast as my legs could move.

Now, Old Campbell, the Scotsman, he didn't scare me like Mummery did but he sure was a crank. If you met him on the street, he'd be nice as pie but in the yard, he'd scowl and be real testy. He had a habit that would shake the section men up. He'd shove his head out of the window of the cab and give them a real ugly look. Campbell's wife, she'd crawl from bed to make him a big lunch to take to work, even if it was 3:00 a.m. She told me that he was a regular Jekyll and Hyde.

"He's one of the finest men there is, until he pulls on his overalls and he becomes a changed man. I don't understand why."

124

Mummery and Campbell. It's funny. Back then, I was so nervous around them but when I remember them now it's with a lot of affection.

Ghost Train

Years ago Bob Twohey was guiding an engine two miles north of the Cochrane yard: the Moosonee Flyer. You have to negotiate through a series of curves and cutbacks to climb the shield. It was eleven at night and he was under orders to link up a bunch of passenger cars at Iroquois Falls for the Moosonee run. Suddenly a huge, blinding spotlight appeared in front of him. He shouted for the fireman, Gus Day, to jump but it was too late. Bob Twohey expected to die.

Then the most amazing thing: the approaching train veered to the right and flashed past the engine, its whistle blowing. The coach windows were lit and he saw passengers looking out. Now, here's the frightening part: there was only a single rail line running through those hills. Gus and he, they took the engine on to Iroquois Falls but didn't tell anyone about the Ghost Train.

They never even talked about it until Bob Twohey went to see a Hungarian fortune-teller in North Bay.

"You must have been drrrinking," she said.

"No we weren't. That's why I came to see you."

"Give me hand, quickly," she ordered.

"Hey!" She'd yanked his arm hard.

"Blessed Virgin protect me," she wailed.

"What?" Bob Twohey exclaimed, rubbing my arm.

"You must leave at once and never return."

"What gives?" he asked.

"I cannot say or we both surely be cursed."

"Come on," he demanded. "I paid good money to have my

fortune told."

"It mean nothing—only ravings of a crazy woman."

"I want to hear my fortune. Now!" He slammed his palm down hard on the table.

"Mother Mary, sanctify us," she sighed. "All right. I tell you, but you regret it for rest of your days."

"Spit it out."

"Your life line—you have one month to live at the most."

Bob Twohey stayed away from trains for a month. But after that, he was back at work. At 8:30 one bright sunny morning, the engine for the Moosonee Flyer was whipping out of Matheson on its way to Cochrane—Jim Nicholson, the engineer, Harry Thompson, the fireman.

It was scheduled to pick up a string of passenger cars and haul them to Moosonee. Now, two miles north of the rail yard, the Flyer came to a high embankment. It had to wind through a series of curves to climb the shield above.

While it was snaking along, a farmer standing at the top of the embankment saw something Nicholson and Thompson couldn't see: another train whizzing down the same railway line a mile away. The farmer waved and hollered.

The fireman reckoned he was just being friendly and he waved back.

Nicholson saw the other train when the Flyer engine reached the plateau.

The passenger train from Timmins with Bob Twohey at the throttle.

Both were travelling at a good clip when they collided. Half the population of North Bay heard it. It was a horrible mess. The Timmins locomotive was thrown off the tracks and the baggage car smashed to smithereens. Seven men were killed, including engineers Nicholson and Twohey.

126

At the inquest, the dispatcher testified that it was Nicholson's fault. He had neglected to check with the Timmins office to learn if the Timmins train had left on time.

Which it hadn't.

Some of Nicholson's co-workers, however, had a different explanation. They said they didn't blame the crash on any mortal being. It was fated to happen. Easy to blame a dead man, of course, and it certainly got the dispatcher off the hook. But no one referred to the Ghost Train at the inquest.

Bob Twohey died five weeks to the day he had his lifeline read.

The Ghost Train hasn't been seen since 1948, but if I had to take a train out of North Bay on a dark night I'd be good and ready to jump.

Eight Hours Of Digging

Late in the winter of 1948 Northern Ontario was clobbered by a blizzard that didn't want to quit. Three months of wind, snow and bitter cold – minus thirty and forty below. The snow drifted as high as telephone poles in open country and was as hard as marble. Farmers rode horses over it without breaking through. No man in his right mind wanted to venture out in that weather. But I was a railroader and when I got the call, I went.

You see, the railway was the life-line for the small towns. Should the roads be plugged and planes couldn't drop supplies, they relied upon us to help them survive. Some folks south of Liskeard needed coal desperately. A train hadn't been by for twelve days. We had three engines and a plough when we left. And eighty diggers. The railway recruited men in beer parlours, cafes and hotel lobbies and paid them 75 cents an hour for shoveling.

Heavens, it was storming that day. I'd been a trainman since 1928, ten years after emigrating from Belgium, and an engineer since '46 and that was the wickedest weather, bar none. You couldn't see ten feet in front of you. They were really hard-up for coal at Latchford. The local citizens heard the engine whistles and made for the station. They had sacks and buckets and anything you could carry coal in. They watched us crack through the drifts north of town.

What a battle. We ran smack into a 25-foot-high drift, solid as the Parthenon. We barged into it and the plough got stuck halfway through. So the diggers went to work. Eighty men shoveled as fast as they could. Eighty hungry men, I might add. We hadn't brought any food with us, and working that hard at that temperature without eating was a terrible ordeal. Eight hours they dug.

We got through alright. We didn't disappoint the people of Latchford.

Marooned

My mom and I were marooned in Northern Ontario in the 1930s. Twenty passengers besides us. It snowed and snowed. It was supposed to be a short trip, and there was no dining car. The only food aboard was the two sandwiches belonging to a school kid. Everyone said they didn't want to take the kid's sandwiches and he should have them himself. That was after six hours. Six hours more, and a committee descended on the kid. For two days we watched the snow blowing on the fields. That night, the conductor left the train and tried to get help, but he had to come back.

"How'd you make out?" the Engineer asked.

"No luck," replied the Conductor shivering and stamping his feet.

"How come?"

"It's tough going. The snow's up to my waist."

"Damn."

"Too bad we don't have any snowshoes," said the Conductor.

"If we did, we would've burned 'em by now. I can't keep the fire going more than two hours then the engine will freeze," said the Engineer grimly.

"Good Lord. Isn't there something we can do?"

"We've burned everything that can burn. Trunks, crates, tables, chairs. You name it. Everything we could scrounge from the baggage car. Hell, the passengers even helped us break up the seats and tear out the wood panels," the Engineer explained.

The Fireman stuck his head in. "I can't keep the fire going without fuel."

"Then the heat will go out!" exclaimed the Conductor.

"It's going to get mighty cold in here – and fast." That was the Fireman.

"If we don't do something soon, we're goners for sure," said the Engineer.

And then I screamed. I was looking out the window and I screamed.

"Elsie!" my mother shouted startled.

"What the hell was that?" asked the Fireman.

"Some scared kid, that's all," said the Engineer.

"Elsie, what's wrong, dear?" my mother asked me.

I pointed out the window. There was something dark, blowing in the snow. Something dark was coming towards the train.

My mother hopped up. "It's all right, Elsie. It's going to be all right," she exclaimed, beckoning the train crew to join her. "Excuse me, gentlemen. I think you better come and look at this."

"Not now, please, ma'am. School girl hysterics will have to take a back seat for now. We're trying to make some critical decisions here," the Conductor grumbled.

"There really is something. Out there!" My mother pointed out the window.

"Yeah. I see it. What the hell is that?" asked the Fireman, pressing his face up against the glass.

"Shh! Listen everyone!" the Conductor shouted.

The sound of sleigh bells in the distance.

A horse pulling a sleigh. And another. One after the other. Farmers in the district knew the train was stuck and they'd ridden out in a blinding blizzard to rescue passengers and crew. They had snacks with them. Apples and preserves from their root-cellars and home-made bread. They couldn't cram many people on the sleighs so they made several trips. Taking them to their farms for hot meals and to let them sit by their kitchen stoves.

Journey's End

The residents of North Bay usually began drifting towards the railway station ten minutes before the evening train was due to arrive. On warm summer nights, or in the freezing grasp of winter, a small band of curious locals wound through the streets to watch the most improbable of entertainment events, the unloading of the 8:15 from Toronto. The merchandise leaving the baggage car was carefully studied to see who was getting what from the T. Eaton Company. A disembarking stranger created speculation and rumour. Was it a new teacher? A hardware salesman? Yet another victim for the foul cooking at Mrs. MacGillivray's boarding house?

As much as anything else, the nightly trek to the North Bay depot, and to many other small-town Northern Ontario stations in the 1920s and 1930s, symbolized the vibrant role the railway once played in this country.

For more than sixty years the railway dominated Northern Ontario and the rest of Canada. Physically, the railroaders tamed 3,000 miles of obstinate land. Spiritually, the train was a familiar constant in a shifting world and, as such, it had an unalterable effect on people's emotions.

The railway brought people from many lands to Northern Ontario in search of fortunes. Diverse cultures fighting diverse weather. They were our pioneers. The railways carried immigrants and fortune-hunters northward and returned with ore and lumber.

Northern Ontarians formed durable friendships, survived savage storms, went to war, drank, honeymooned, and, occasionally gave birth on trains. They even in fell in love on them.

To have a railway man in your family was a reason to be proud; engineers and conductors were almost as glamorous as hockey players.

"Whooo-Oooo-Oooo!"

Hear that? That's history being made. June 25, 1957. The end of an era. ONR Steam Engine 701 from Timmins pulling in to the CPR station at North Bay for the last time. I think the whole *North Bay Nugget* staff was there: two reporters and a photographer on the train. The big event. They've already got the headline written: "A Farewell to Steam—Victim of Progress."

By the end of the steam era's heyday, branch lines spoked out from every major centre, reaching villages and towns where, if roads to communities existed at all, they were torturous bush trails. But the leapfrogging popularity of the automobile and the airliner after the Second World War had seriously weakened the trains' hold on our national consciousness. In the post-war boom, there were more highways and more people could afford cars.

In the years that followed, the Ontario Northland Railroad, like all railways, made a few sputtering attempts to fight the competition, claiming it lacked the money to do a proper job.

131

A hot summer night.
The middle of July, 3:00 a.m.
In the distance the sound of that lonely train whistle.
That's the last sound I hope to hear the moment before I die.

Editor's note:
Rod Carley conducted a series of informal interviews with retired Northern Ontario railroaders and passengers in 1999. These interviews became the basis for the original musical, *Train Town*, presented by the Nipissing Stage Company in North Bay in 2000. Rod was the founding Artistic Director of the Nipissing Stage Company (NSC) from 1999 to 2005. Part of the NSC's mandate was to create an original musical each season documenting the heritage and history of Northern Ontario.

The final Northlander passenger train pulled out of the North Bay station on September 28th, 2012, bringing more than a century of passenger rail history to an end.

Literacy, Alfred Fitzpatrick and My Vocation in Algoma

By Evelyn C. Diebel

"Wherever and Whenever (people) have occasion to congregate, then and there shall be a time, place, and means of their education."
Alfred Fitzpatrick, 1920

There is no place I'd rather be outside my home than in a library. Just being in the Marie Michael Library at the Coady International Institute in the summer of 2016 was a privilege. Along with my classmates, I was giddy to be studying in this particular library, located on the campus of St. Francis Xavier University, Antigonish, Nova Scotia, with its books containing knowledge on social movements that transformed Canada and improved the quality of adult learning within the country, such as the The Antigonish Movement, The Women's Institute and Frontier College. It surpassed my expectations. My class was melded with experienced students from all over Canada and various parts of Africa. I must admit, I was feeling somewhat out of sorts being from a little Northern Ontario town. Our initial group work divided us into groups to work on the specific timeline of adult education in Canada.

"Hey, Evelyn, aren't you from Nairn Centre?" I heard one of

my classmates say as she read my name tag. It was then I learned Nairn Centre was the location of the first established reading camp in Canada.

What a revelation it was for me to discover the little town where I had lived for the past 29 years, where we raised our three kids, was at the very beginning of the timeline of adult education in Canada. How unforeseen—the small town of Nairn Centre "Algoma" was the First Reading Camp in Canada, established in 1899 by Alfred Fitzpatrick. I felt pleased, proud, and curious all at the same time.

I began the journey of getting to know just who Alfred Fitzpatrick was and what his vocation and life's work meant to him; and more specifically why he chose Nairn Centre as part of his assessment of adult educational needs. I began to ask some critical questions to find out important facts. I compared our thoughts, measuring the strategies we both used in adult education. Was his vocation and my life experiences intertwining and leading me to learn more about the story of his life's work?

When I was a little girl, growing up in the small pulp and paper town of Espanola, just west of Nairn Centre, we lived across the street from my mother's French speaking parents. I attended a small French Catholic school and had everything I needed. My maternal grandparents were at the centre of my being. My grandmother and grandfather had a miniature bookcase, or library, in their home. I was so intrigued by those books that I started to catalogue them, forcing my younger brother to play "Let's go to the library". I, of course, was the librarian. Those books smelled musty but the text on yellowed parchment paper intrigued me. I was certain that my grandparents had never read them. My grandfather could not read. My grandmother read a little more than he, yet the books were obviously valued.

As a child, I also remember going to the grocery store with my mother every week, not because I was interested in shopping for food and household goods, or to help her out, but for the books. Tucked into the produce section, there was a small carousel of books, geared for various ages. She would always allow me to choose one every week. I devoured the words, knowledge, and would reread it over and over again. I would then write about it in my journal and anticipate the following week's store visit to add another book to my collection. My mother preserved those books with a "mack tack" clear cover. My collection of books, both French and English, and journals grew over the years, and still, to this day, I have those books and many more. I love being surrounded by books. I realized at a very young age that it is never too late for anyone to follow through on education.

I was a stay-at home mother for fifteen years and books were my companion everywhere I went. Whether I was reading to my children, indulging in a novel while they were asleep, or simply skimming a few pages with some tea in the afternoon while the boys played in the backyard, books were always there. When the twins were one year old, I began to engage in university level distance education courses and they required a lot of reading. It was not easy to juggle being a wife, mother and student during those early years in Nairn Centre. I did, however, find a like-minded group of women in the neighbouring community of Beaver Lake at a toy lending library program. These educated women made a conscientious decision to stay at home with their children too.

Over the years, we enjoyed each other's company and when our children started going to school, we formed a book club so we could continue sharing recipes, parentings ideas, knowledge on homemaking and books, many, many books over the years. That was twenty-two years ago. The sharing circle of book club evenings, snacks, and cakes has enriched my life tremendously. The love and support of these women remains invaluable to me. We are, and will forever be, linked by friendship, experiences, and books.

As an adult educator myself, I felt a kinship, in spirit, with the man who came to my community so long ago to bring books and education. I had to honour his work by educating our small town of less that 500 people about his contribution. It was part of my continuous educational vocation. I had to gather more information and find out for myself about this historical gem found at the Antigonish institute.

With my community building experiences and relationships I had made over the years, I needed to get to the grassroots and learn more. I engaged in conversations with elders, searched for books, read information online, and reached out to Frontier College, which is the institute founded over a century ago by Mr. Fitzpatrick to promote adult literacy.

From about 1890, and for two decades into the next century, the economic mainstay of this area was logging with a direct connection to a lumber mill in Nairn Centre—the same mill that employed my own husband as a lumber grader for twenty-two years. I learned that the town of Nelsonville was at the Nairn train station, one of the first buildings to be erected in Nairn. It was a large two-story frame building with vast living quarters attached to the office, waiting room and freight shed. This building was heated by five wood stoves, using an enormous amount of coal and wood supplied by the C.P.R. With no electricity, oil lamps and lanterns were the standard source of light. In 1896, the people decided to be formally recognized as a community. The community would have to decide on who their first officials were going to be and since they had to pick a name for their town they decided to pick Nairn Centre.

Like me, Alfred Fitzpatrick was inspired by books and innovative education when he was growing up in rural Nova Scotia. He knew sacrifices had to be made in order to become "educated"

EVELYN C. DIEBEL

and he believed in innovative education. Alfred was born in the farming community of Millsville, in Pictou County in 1862. He was raised in a family that knew the values of hard work, education and service to humanity. He came from a close-knit Scots-Irish background, and he was the second youngest of twelve children. I imagine he was a well-disciplined and hardworking child. He attended Pictou Academy and then moved to Kingston, Ontario where he obtained an arts degree. He went on to study theology and became an ordained Presbyterian minister. Rev. Alfred Fitzpatrick graduated from Queen's College in 1892.

At Queen's, he became acquainted with extension education activity and emergent Social Gospel beliefs anticipated by its renowned Principal, George Monro Grant. Fitzpatrick was influenced, but not ruled, by the liberal Protestant view seeking to impart the social relevance of religion. Proponents of the Social Gospel considered social welfare for the working class to be as important as spiritual salvation. They emphasized a broader collective responsibility for church work to counter the sins of society in general. Individual self-improvement and elevated moral standards among all classes could build self-respect and contribute to the fellowship of man. Fitzpatrick took particular interest in using books to encourage literacy in order to offer better working conditions, personal advancement for "camp men", and good citizens for society. The young minister had worked and gained experience in rural lumber camps in California, New Brunswick, and Saskatchewan before taking up his new charge in 1899 at Nairn Centre, a small village southwest of Sudbury, Ontario.

People in the work camps and other transient labourers were a major part of the Canadian national reality. During this time, many of the workers were employed at the first level of Canadian industry. They extracted coal, iron, gold, and the lumber for construction of the necessary transportation systems of rail and road

150 YEARS UP NORTH AND MORE

to bring these raw resources to the factories, refineries and sawmills. These workers were unrepresented and non-unionized, existing as a tertiary labour force in the mines, forests and railway construction gangs. Their working conditions were appalling, their living conditions were primitive. Their prospects for education and improved working conditions were non-existent.

In mid-February 1899, the young minister and educator, Alfred Fitzpatrick, boarded a train in Toronto bound for the community of Nairn Centre in Northern Ontario. The train headed west and then stopped in the middle of a lonely stretch of tracks, almost twenty hours later. It was cold, but even the northern chill of February had not dampened his spirits or those of the volunteers accompanying him. With snowshoes and lanterns to find their way, they set out to bring the good news and opportunity to those who needed it the most. When they arrived, just after dawn, the camp was empty. The loggers were already at work. By the time the men returned that evening, they found something new in their rough settlement—a tent. But it was not just any tent. A large banner on the tent proclaimed: Reading Tent: All Welcome!

When I hear the train whistle, at any hour of day or night in my community, I cannot help but stop and think of the courage and knowledge Fitzpatrick had on his journey to "Algoma" - Nairn Centre. Alfred Fitzpatrick and his volunteers sat in the tent at tables piled high with books of poetry, history, mathematics and philosophy. He believed education should be accessible on the farm, bush, railway or mine.

Fitzpatrick said, "We must educate the whole family wherever their work is, wherever they earn their living; teaching them how to earn and at the same time how to grow physically, intellectually, and spiritually to the full stature of their God-given potentialities. This is the real education. This is the place of the true university."

Fitzpatrick developed the idea of the Labourer-Teacher who

works alongside the labourers during the day and teaches them in the evenings. In these early days, Frontier College managed its work largely though volunteers. The college's young instructor by the name of Angus Gray contrived the title Labourer-Teacher. He was bored with waiting for the men at Hall's Lumber Camp, near Nairn Centre, to return to the reading tent after a day's work, so he picked up an axe and went out to join the men in the forest. The gesture helped to establish a natural connection between instructor and worker. By 1903 and 1904, all reading camp instructors became Labourer-Teachers, and their reports from the field reflected this. It offered thousands of young people the opportunity to move into the outlying communities and camps and, once there, to support themselves by working side by side with the workers; and then, the end of the shift, the workers would become their students. Fitzpatrick respected the physical labour woodsmen performed, and was determined to advance their well-being, believing traditional missionary service that supplied Indigenous and isolated communities with religious and self-help work was inadequate. Fitzpatrick's mission was simple: education for all. Every Canadian, not just a privileged few must have access to basic education and the opportunity to study at the university level. "Bring education to the people, not the people to education."

The Canadian Reading Camp Movement was established in 1899, and by 1903 there were twenty-four reading rooms in various locations, constructed as permanent log structures or simply as portable prospector's tents. The books were provided by the Ontario Development of Education travelling libraries. Church congregations provided magazines and newspapers. Fitzpatrick also contributed financially to the cause.

In 1919, the Reading Camp Association was preparing for the anticipated new wave of migrant labour with the end of the war in Europe. Fitzpatrick had anticipated this wave of migration for some time and wanted to be prepared for an influx of labourers to trickle into the camps. It would mean additional funding to support Labourer-Teachers in more camps. The camps would receive many more labourers who would require not only education, but a good sense of "Canadianization" in the work camps.

After many years of compiling his ideas and contributions to adult education for adults, Fitzpatrick produced a *Handbook for New Canadians*. This book could be used today as a resource in my adult literacy classroom. The hardcover textbook contains a series of lessons in English with considerable practical information about Canada. Hand illustrations and photographs are accompanied by a stock word list for the adult learner; a visual to accompany the phonetics and words. His chapters are specifically labeled on subjects such as Canadian history and government, naturalization and basic English language structure. The influx of non-English-speaking people into Canada at the time was very large in proportion to the population. Fitzpatrick believed immigrants must take pride in the land they chose and wanted to help them get acquainted with the language, customs and laws of their new home country.

At the back of the *Handbook for New Canadians* there is a 700 word vocabulary in Italian, French, Swedish, Ukrainian, Russian, Yiddish and English. This resource provided both the instructor and immigrant with a communication tool that proved to be an essential aid for better understanding of everyday conversation in various languages.

Over the years, Fitzpatrick made a strong plea to the government to recognize Frontier College. He delineated in his book, *University in Overalls: A Plea for Part-Time Study* (1920), how the universities could convert "the whole industrial world into a university". In 1922, Frontier College was granted a Dominion Charter. His perseverance, his time, energy, intellect, and vision were brought forward as an alternative way of learning and attaining education.

He established literacy programs to promote reading among the young, education and literacy to labourers, remote communities, people with learning disabilities, and marginalized populations.

Alfred Fitzpatrick died in 1936, and his vocation to bring education to the people is now continuing through the everyday efforts of Frontier College, its many volunteers, and existing programs. His vocation also lives on in each and every one of us that have the occasion to congregate and learn from each other and in our life experiences. On June 22, 2017, with the support of the Nairn-Hyman Township Town Council, community members, OK Signs, and Frontier College, a banner honouring Alfred Fitzpatrick and recognizing Nairn Centre as 'Canada's First Reading Camp' was placed at both entrances of this historic town that I now know, and that I call home.

Living with Grandmother
By Lee Weimer*

*Based on an autobiographical sketch of Kateri Jackson from Wikwemikong, ON

Sleeping, I tucked myself into the warm, soft spot of Grandmother's backside. It was a wonderful feeling to know I could sleep safe in Grandmother's house. I could let all my anxious thoughts and fears slip away into a peaceful river of darkness.

Sometime during the night, I could sense Grandmother get up; the bed springs would move ever so gently, but I was not worried because I knew her routine and that soon she would be back, all snuggled into the blankets. And I could dream on, uninterrupted, into a bliss that was almost heaven.

I was happy living with Grandmother, me and my two sisters. I don't want to say anything that would intentionally hurt their feelings because I love them but I felt that I was Grandmother's favourite. I was also the oldest.

Living with Grandmother, I got to know all her little character traits: her likes and her not likes. It was Grandmother's way, every morning to roll her long, white hair into a tight, neat bun, put on her old print dress that came to her ankles, tie on her apron and get to work. There was so much work to do and we all had our chores, even us little girls. Grandmother would send us out to the woodpile, beside the barn. We would pick up one or two pieces of wood and bring it in for the wood stove. At other times, I would go to the well that was in the yard, throw down the pail that was tied to the rope and when I heard it splash, I'd begin to haul it up, full of water. That was hard work. The rope was rough and hurt my hands. But Grandmother needed the water to make porridge for breakfast. We were always hungry and had good appetites.

Maybe Grandmother wasn't as fashionable as other grand-mothers but she was the only one I knew and for me, the deep wrinkles in her smile told me I was loved. She was my best friend.

Grandmother's other family included my Dad, his younger brother and two baby sisters. They had all grown up long ago but now she called us her little blessings, come to cheer her up on the last part of her journey.

We all lived in Grandmother's house. It was covered in imita-tion blue tarpaper that was made to look like bricks. There was a kitchen and sitting room on the main floor. Upstairs, there was one big sleeping room. I felt so cozy and safe, sleeping together, in that room.

There were other houses and other families, our neighbours, who lived on that same dirt road. The road followed the shore-line and then went up the bluff to the cemetery. We named this place Dooganing, because it described how the land opened up to the sky, filled with low lying willows and marshy shallows. But it was hard to say when you didn't know the Anishnaabehmowin language, so later on, everyone called it South Bay. It was a place the Pottawatomi people settled after they had to leave their homes on the upper Michigan peninsula after the War of 1812.

South Bay was a small little community far from the main village of Wikwemikong. I was too young to make the full day journey over there, walking on that long and thirsty road, but many people did go visiting relatives and friends.

Wikwemikong has always been the largest community on the reserve. Some say, long ago, there was a large colony of beavers that lived in the bay where the settlement first got started.

It's easy to see how using the root word *amik*, from the Anishnaabek word for beaver, in the naming of Wi- kwemik- ong would be a natural thing to do.

There was nothing much to look at when you did get there: just another dusty dirt road, winding along the shore. There were more houses and more people, more possibilities to meet up with other people, but I've begun to notice how people seem to get friendlier when you don't see them so often.

Most everyone would take some time to stop and visit at Andy's. He had opened up his front room to sell bread, jam, canned milk, boxes of chocolates and other smaller items that you had forgotten to buy at the better stocked general stores in Manitouwaning. Better still, he dealt in credit.

He was in a prime location, right at the corner of an intersection with the main road. He and his family opened up for business from early morning to late at night. Everyone seemed to sit around his front porch, sharing the news. There simply was no other place to go. It was also the last stop before climbing the hill to the church.

The most important and most impressive building in the village sat right on top of the hill. It was the Holy Cross Mission Church, built by the parishioners for the Jesuit Fathers. The mission had its beginnings when M'nidoo Minis (Manitoulin Island) was mostly made up of Odawa, Pottawatomi and Ojibwe peoples. The first mention of any visiting Jesuit priests was during the exploration voyages of Samuel de Champlain, First Governor of New France

(1601), who brought with him a Catholic zeal for converting the innocents. It didn't take long for the French Pères to start their own migrations into the new colony of Quebec. They continued to open up the mission field across the great lakes and westward. By 1648 they had established contact at Wikwemikong that has endured to this present day.

Minidoowaaing was a name given to a very special and sacred place. This place was home of the Great Spirit Serpent who lived in a deep underwater cave at the very bottom of Minidoowaaing Bay. But that is a story Grandmother told on cold winter nights when the frost inside the windows made snowflake patterns so thick you had to scratch a peephole to look outside.

Manitouwaning became the name of the village that was settled in this area. It was also the farthest place that I travelled with Grandmother. She usually asked her brother John to drive us over there in his old Chevrolet. She made sure everyone was treated equal. All us girls got to go into the village once a month. I remember the thrill of those car rides. Especially the doors. They weren't the same as in other cars. Something magical happened when they opened out all together. It looked so big and grand. I felt like stepping into a princess' coach. Uncle John's car was unique. It was the only one in our neighbourhood.

The journey to Manitouwaning seemed to take forever and that was alright with me. I loved car rides, looking out the window, looking at the different colours, seeing anyone walking on the road passing by. The road took us off the reserve. Grandmother said at one time there was a gate on that road where the reserve land ended. It used to be you needed a pass from the Indian agent to leave. He was the only one to give you that permission slip to get off our land. Everyone was under his control, if he didn't like you he could make life harder, to trade or go to work elsewhere. There was that gate and he was the gatekeeper.

145

Grandmother says things began to change after the veterans came back from the second great war overseas. It wasn't long after that the gate was taken down.

The Lieutenant-Governor of Upper Canada, Sir Francis Bondhead, came to Manitouwaning in 1836 to attend ceremonies for the distribution of presents as part of previous treaty negotiations. He asked for a council meeting with the chiefs to designate Manitoulin Island as a place of refuge for native people.

A proclamation was signed stating the native people could keep their land. Many of the chiefs did not write the English language so they made their mark on the paper instead, to be polite. They already knew this land belonged to them. But things don't turn out the way you expect them to. It usually doesn't for us. It usually gets worse.

It wasn't long before the government decided to get involved with the Anglican Church to build a school and a church in Manitouwaning. It was intended as a place to learn a different way of life. The old ways of living off the land were gone. We could no longer fish, hunt, harvest wild rice or pick berries in season without being charged with trespassing.

The school eventually closed down and the native people left. It became a place where other people came to live. They came after the government sent men to survey our land for sale. This was in Grandmother's mother's time. A time of deep sorrow and neglect. Families became separated because they didn't understand the new rules of living with the white families coming to settle here. After a while, we did go visiting these descendants but as they were not related to us, we could not understand them. They didn't speak like us. Most of these families came from far away across the seas, from countries I could not name. England, Scotland and Ireland were all part of the British Empire.

Owen Maguire's family came from Scotland, near Glasgow.

146

They bought land to farm in Bidwell Township: a wild, untamed piece of wilderness of cedar swamps and rocky hillocks. It was also home to a large deer and mosquito population. They eventually moved out to Hilly Grove where they built a solid brick house. Owen, always a quiet man, and for that reason trusted to keep his own counsel. He came to know Grandmother when he opened Maguire's Hardware Store.

It may have been that Grandmother's heart quickened when she met Owen. And I have to wonder, years later, if she didn't get that call box put in the kitchen just to crank it up and whisper his name, "Ow'n, is that you?"

In those days, flour came in good quality cotton sacks, decorated in pretty floral patterns. A perfect fit for a new dress. Years ago, Grandmother had bought an old fashioned treadle sewing machine, a Singer that clicked and clacked long into the night. The next day, I would be the happiest girl in South Bay. I had a new dress to wear. I always kept checking the flour bin and looked forward to the day when there would be nothing left but dust. I knew then it wouldn't be too long before we would be making a trip to Manitouwaning to buy more. Grandmother always seemed to know how much was left in the monthly allowance we were given by the government agent.

There was no money. I guess Indians couldn't be trusted to count it. There was a system of vouchers. First, a band councillor had to approve the request, then the Indian agent in Manitouwaning would sign the voucher which Grandmother then took to the store. At one time there were five general stores, three gas stations, two hotels and other businesses in Manitouwaning. It was busily being prosperous.

Grandmother went to McPhee's General Store. We were served one by one. I wonder now if that was a standard practice for everyone or just for us. It was very quiet and still in there, absolutely no talking. My eyes could just look over one of the two long wooden counters that ran along each side of the room. Behind the counter, there were endless shelves stacked to the ceiling with all kinds of food, material, dolls and other wonderful things.

Grandmother would give her order to the woman standing at the counter; five pounds of bacon, ten pounds of sugar, two pounds of beans, maybe a tin of peaches, a pail of lard, some baking powder, yeast and a big 25 lb bag of flour. Sometimes at the very end of her order she would ask for a few sticks of hard candy. Everything was wrapped in brown paper, tied up with the string that twirled from a large spool suspended over the counter. It was an amazing thing to watch when it was pulled down and wrapped around the packages. I knew Grandmother would save the string to use for other things.

There was always time to visit Maguire's Hardware Store right across the street. Owen was never in a hurry when he greeted us. We could walk up and down the aisles, looking and touching whatever was on the shelves.

My small, little world of open fields, creeks and woods that was our farm was interrupted one day, when Grandmother decided that I could go and work for Mrs. MacKinnon on Saturdays. I couldn't believe the excitement. Grandmother was very strict. She wouldn't allow any of us to go anywhere without someone to watch over us. But she had worked for Mrs. MacKinnon years ago and so I went.

I put on my new flowered dress and waited for 8:00 a.m. when Uncle John would drive me out to the main highway, past Manitouwaning, to her home. I felt so growed up when I opened the door of his car, to sit on upholstered seats, roll down the window, and day dream all the way there. We would bump along the ruts in the dirt road, making huge dust clouds behind us and that was fun too.

I remember the first time we drove into her lane. Trees shaded the long driveway with branches overlapping each other. It looked like a picture I once saw in a book.

Mrs. MacKinnon was a busy woman. Years ago, she had gone away to nursing school in the city. Her husband was more reserved and thoughtful. He could watch molasses drip from a spoon and still be impressed.

Most days Mr. MacKinnon would give me the day's chores to do, outside. I would feed the chickens, collect eggs, weed the garden, pick vegetables, anything a twelve year old could do. But one time he said the house needed painting. I just looked at him. I'd never painted a house before. He put a can of paint on top of the ladder and gave me a brush. Of course, I climbed up on that ladder and I got started. I can't really remember how that job ended. I guess farm work is like that. You do what you have to do.

The farm had a lot of animals. There were chickens, pigs, cows and sheep. The little lambs were the cutest. Mr. MacKinnon would give me bottles filled with milk to feed them in my arms when their own mothers couldn't do it. They were so cute and woolly and soft.

The day Mr. MacKinnon needed help with the sheep and asked me to help, I'll never forget. It seemed their tails needed to be cut off. I was to hold their tails steady over a chopping block while he did the chopping. There was so much blood, all over me and the ground and on the sheep. I was afraid of the axe but I didn't dare cry. I don't remember anything much more of that day. I guess I had to get cleaned up in the mudroom before coming into the kitchen for lunch.

Mrs. MacKinnon didn't seem to think anything was wrong. I sat down at the kitchen table and she served me my favourite lunch, Campbell's Vegetable soup and a tomato sandwich with lettuce on white French stick bread. This was a luxury we could never afford at home. I would have gladly come and worked for her for free, just to have that lunch. But I didn't tell her that. She paid me $5.00 for the day. I worked from 9:00am until dusk when Uncle John would come for me. Grandmother told me to give him the money and I did.

I didn't realize my last day working for Mrs. MacKinnon's would end so suddenly. After I had worked a full day for her, instead of giving me the $5.00, she gave me a picture of three oxen ploughing in a field. It was strange that such a large picture had no glass even though the frame was made of carved wood and was very heavy.

I came home with this picture and showed Grandmother. She was furious. The next Saturday she called Mrs. MacKinnon and told her I would not be coming back. I never saw Mrs. MacKinnon again.

It wasn't until later that I learned Mrs. MacKinnon was Owen Maguire's sister.

The Hotel
By Sarah McComb

"This is the spot?" I call over to my grandfather, and he nods in return. I wait to feel it—that nostalgic pull, passed down through generations, rooting me here.

I kind of do. Or maybe it's the melancholy of the grey sky, the smell of the Sault Ste. Marie steel plant hanging in the air.

I pick my way over cracked cement. In front of me is a furniture store. To my left is what used to be an intersection, now cobble-stoned over, blocked off, and lined with decorative boulders.

And where I'm standing used to be a hotel. Or, as my family refers to it, *The Hotel*.

"This here was the entrance," says my grandfather. His steps are careful, slow, and deliberate, picking his way around weeds and shards of broken glass. "One door for the men, one door for the women. And this was the lobby. My old man used to sit there and talk to everyone going through."

As we walk through the lot, he fills in more of what used to be here. The fire escape that helped his brother sneak in and out of the building. The kitchen where they held their Sunday dinners; boarders and family members sitting around the same giant table.

The bar, filled with smoke, pool games, laughter; and before prohibition was lifted, illicit moonshine.

The building rises up in front of me, layer after layer of stories about the New Toronto Hotel and my great-grandfather, passed down from relatives and friends. This was the place that rooted my family in this city, that still shapes them today, that every reminiscing session turns towards.

When I want to look back at my family's history everyone points me here. And I'm determined to grasp as much of that history as I can, before it all dissipates like dust in the air after a demolition.

They tore the hotel down decades ago, and now there's nothing left but the outline against the building next door and newer concrete where they filled in the basement. Nothing but empty air in the shape of what used to be there.

My grandfather stands with his hands clasped behind his back, formal, the way I've seen his father stand in pictures. With his tweed jacket and the brim of his hat pulled down low, he looks like he's stepped out of time.

"It was all here," he says. "It looks so small now."

When my great-grandfather, Joko Culina, stepped off the ship in Halifax, the first thing he noticed was the ground—the way it rolled under his feet like he was still on the water. He was at the edge of his new country, possibility stretching out as far as he could see.

The trip over would have felt endless. He had spent a week crammed into steerage, listening to the thunder of the engines and the water. Everyone slept stacked in bunks without sheets, jostled for food, staggered into each other with the motion of the waves. He had only one familiar face on the ship: a man from the same village, older than his father.

His older brother had already arrived in North America a few years before, and he'd settled in New York State. But Canada—Canada all belonged to Joko. Around him was the sound of gulls, the sting of sleet, the smell of salt, and a chorus of voices speaking in a language he did not yet understand. He'd made it—from the village his family had lived in for centuries, across an ocean, to the cusp of his new life.

He was sixteen, then. I imagine he was fleeing political tensions and the looming threat of war in the Balkans. Or maybe he had gotten into trouble with the law in the old country. Either way, he wanted a fresh start. So, when they asked for his name, he gave them his little brother's. He used it as his own, as a stepping stone to a new world.

After he landed in Halifax, he moved to Niagara Falls for eight years; a time in his life that he never spoke about. And for eight years, the only trace of him I have is paperwork from a failed border crossing to the American side, *debarred* stamped across the bottom in blurry, black ink.

"Do you know what this was about?" I asked my grandfather, handing him a photocopy of the record. "He got turned away from the States."

My grandfather shook his head, then pulled out his reading glasses and peered closer at the spidery handwriting. "I didn't know he lived in Niagara Falls," he said.

The more I researched, the more it started to take shape. At the border, the agent would have had questions—about Joko's reasons for entering the States, about his identity. With his stubborn streak and his limited English, mainly cobbled together from the manual labour jobs he picked up, things got heated.

He was pulled aside. He was detained. And he was brought before a tribunal.

They quizzed him about the purpose of his trip, his identifying

153

information, his life's story. With limited border security, he should have been able to confirm his identity, establish that he was off to visit his brother for the day, and continue on his way. A hassle, but an easily-solved one.

But my great-grandfather had a dislike of authority and a penchant for giving different names—Jure, Jozo, Josip. He was proud, defiant, and tired, coming up against a committee that pressed him for more and more answers. He had ten dollars in his pocket. He was never one to follow a law he didn't agree with, so he probably had some flasks of moonshine on him, too. And if he had moonshine on him, I'd like to think he offered the tribunal a drink, half out of bribery and half out of spite.

At the end of all of it, he was denied entry into the United States and sent back to Canada.

Border crossing difficulties aside, his first year in Canada must have been incredible. He would have seen 'the falls', but not so many times that the wonderment wore off. In later years, he would choose the waterfall background when he had his family portraits taken, so he was impressed with the beauty of the scenery, the thunderous rushing of the water. Maybe he sent touristy postcards and pictures back to his family in Croatia—although since he could not read nor write, he would have needed to find someone to dictate things to.

And that first winter—after arriving with no winter clothes, having never seen snow before, and being thrown into an average temperature of seven below — he would have wondered how much colder it could possibly get. Growing up in the balmy climate of the Adriatic Coast, he wouldn't have ever seen that much snow at once. I imagine he thought he'd moved to a frozen hellscape; that he'd never get warm.

In his later years, once he had retired, he would go sunbathing along the shores of the St. Mary's River, watching the freighters go past on their way to and from the locks. Even in the heat of August, he would wear thermal underwear.

Somewhere along the line, he heard of Sault Ste. Marie, and he traded one Ontario border town for another. And he got married.

His photo from his first wedding hangs in my hallway. It's still in the ornate wooden frame it came in, and the image has barely so much as faded with time. He and his wife have that standard 1920s solemn look on their faces, although his is more proud and hers is more baleful. The picture is in black and white, with details added and enhanced with thin brush strokes.

The colorizing probably came with the photography services. But I'd like to think it was also a bit of his own decision, giving his wife a splash of pink shoelaces to liven up the grey of the photo, adding some jewelry over the white silk of her gloves, colouring in the dark brown of his own hair.

His passport claimed his height to be five foot ten, a good half foot too generous if old photos are anything to go by. He must have bribed someone at the counter when he applied, or perhaps he had a family member rewrite the numbers after he brought the document home. In an age when national security was not a looming spectre over everything, it seemed no one cared that he wasn't as tall as he said.

At the steel plant in Sault Ste. Marie, he earned the nickname Jumbo, not for height reasons but because of his strength. Stubborn and sturdy, he could do the lifting of two men—or more, if you believe the legend-like stories people told about him. While the steel plant churned out railway tracks, he learned how to swear in Italian, and he did the heavy lifting.

But working at the steel plant wasn't his goal. He'd spent years as a labourer, but he wanted something more to show for his life in Canada, something that people would remember him by. He and a business partner—a man who came from the same village in Croatia and worked at the steel plant with him—started their own business on the corner of James and Cathcart streets. First, it was a dry goods store and arcade. Second, a public bathing facility. Third, a boarding house. Finally, a hotel and bar: The New Toronto.

The Hotel.

They named it the New Toronto to put it in direct competition with the New Ontario a short distance away. But the city provided a fitting namesake, too, for their ability to fit so many people in one space. Between my great-grandfather and his business partner, their families numbered four adults and as many as nine kids at once—and that wasn't including the guests and the regulars who stayed there.

And there were regulars. People looking for an inexpensive room, or workers from the steel plant. Almost all of them were Croatians who found each other in Northern Ontario. Back then, the boarding houses seemed to fall along country lines, with the clientele being all from Croatia, or Ukraine, or Italy, depending on the nationality of the owner. At the New Toronto, they all ate Sunday dinners together in the dining room. Blood-related or not, they were a family.

One nephew stayed on his way to enlist in the war. He brought his guitar with him, and he sat cross-legged on the bed, playing... except that he didn't know how to play the instrument to begin with, so his attempt at a song involved plucking one string over and over in perfect time. He was there for two weeks, driving his cousins up the wall with his constant attempts at music. And then he shipped out, leaving the building a little quieter.

They got a pool table, and a shuffleboard table. There was music—tamburicas, accordions, bass, and so much singing. There was food, a hodgepodge of Croatian, Ukrainian, Polish, and Italian cuisine—meals brought from the old country and picked up from their new neighbours. There was moonshine and wine brewing in the basement, and a crowd of people waiting upstairs to drink it. It wasn't always smooth going, of course. In the early 1930s, a fire roared through their block on James Street. After the smoke had cleared and the buildings had cooled, Joko took a piece of glass and pressed it into his four-year-old son's hands. Kneeling on the ground next to him, he showed him how to scrape the charred layers of wood from the floor without cutting himself. His son remembered hours of scraping with little to show for his efforts, the boards stubbornly black beneath his hands.

Fires were common then; calls to the fire department were rare. There were stories of people taking care of everything themselves as best they could, heaving burning furniture out of open windows to burn on their front lawn. No one wanted to call in the firefighters because no one wanted them to discover the stills inside.

He would keep on putting his kids to work, too. Once they became old enough to take orders and mix drinks, his sons worked at the bar. They kept one eye on the door for police officers, ready to drop to the ground and hide behind the counter if any came in, not wanting to get in trouble for being too young to serve booze. One son took over the bar as he got older; the other refused after a drunken patron threw a brick at his head. "I quit," he'd roared at his father, the broken pieces still on the ground behind him.

His wife's death certificate says *goiter*, but thyroid trouble was unlikely to be lethal that quickly. She sickened and passed away suddenly, and there he was, with a hotel to run and five young children grieving for their mother.

His business partner's wife took over many of the parenting duties, and his kids started to think of her as a sort of mother. But it was a lot of young children to handle, and he tried to figure out a solution.

His wife's sister, newly widowed, still lived in Croatia. He wrote to her—dictated, then signed with the X he used in place of his name—and suggested a marriage. She could move to Canada, he wrote. The only thing was, she would have to leave one of her children behind. Her son, she could bring. Her daughter would have to stay in Europe.

His children already slept as many as four to a bed, crammed in sideways in order to take advantage of as much mattress space as they could, sticking their cold feet against each other's backs. And he already had two daughters at home. He had to be realistic, he reasoned, about how much his family could grow.

And as callous as the proposal sounded, the wait to hear back from her must have been agonizing.

His youngest child had sickened. In the only photo I have of him, he's barely a toddler. He's crying, trying to push himself out of his father's arms, and staring straight into the camera. His squirming makes him look blurry and eerie. It's like he's looking through time and he knows what's going to happen; like his life is somehow less fixed in place.

When her response finally arrived in the mail, Joko must have brought it to a friend to read to him. He must have been nervous as he ripped open the envelope. He was grabbing at this last chance to bring his kids a bit of their mother over from Europe.

But she refused to marry him.

And his youngest son died.

And then, he gave away his youngest daughter to be raised by her uncle and aunt in New York. They had requested a son; my great-grandfather refused.

Finally, in desperation, he got a mail order bride sent from Croatia, a complete stranger to help hold together what remained

158

of his family.

Even though he married someone else, he sent money to his wife's sister. When she turned down his proposal, it must have been a terrible decision to have to make. Whether it was because she didn't want to move to Canada, or because she couldn't bear to leave her daughter behind, she now faced the prospect of a lifetime of poverty and war. But he took care of her as best he could, sending whatever money he was able, even if it wasn't a lot. And when my grandfather started making money for himself, Joko sat him down and said, "You'll send money to your aunt."

My grandfather gave him a startled look. He spent his summers in the States, helping his aunt and uncle with the hotel they ran. He worked for free, promised that they would remember him in their wills. "What aunt? The one in Buffalo?" As his father explained, my grandfather realized that this was the first he'd heard of her. A whole side of the family that Joko had been quietly supporting for years.

On himself, my great-grandfather wouldn't spend money. He didn't buy new clothes unless he could help it. He grew his own vegetables, and he brewed his own liquor. When he travelled, he brought his own cold cuts, bread, and cheese, enough to eat for every meal while he was away. He stayed in the cheapest of accommodations. And if you asked him how he slept the next morning, he would answer, "No good." With a loud snort, he would add, "Pffft, too expensive."

On other people, it was a different story. He sponsored family and friends from Croatia to come to Canada. When a relative of his wife's was sick and staying in a rival hotel, he would send his children over with free, home-cooked meals anyway. He did things like that, often and without fanfare. And he impressed on his children the importance of doing the same.

He lived in the West End, in the Little Italy part of town. Violence and intimidation were common, especially aimed at Italian families. For a few terrible years, there were cross burnings, and one of the common locations was across from a nearby church. It was close enough that Joko would have seen the flames out his windows.

There was a line through the middle of the city, Gore Street, that divided the European immigrants in the west from the British immigrants in the east. And anyone who crossed Gore Street going east risked getting jumped.

But not his son. His son was a jock, a hotshot football player for his high school team. When he had to miss a game after getting his tonsils out, his absence made the sports headlines in the *Sault Star*. Joko had a neighbour come over and read the football articles to him while he glowed with pride. He wouldn't let on to his son, though. He didn't want his son to stop striving to be *better*, to achieve *more*.

His son could cross Gore Street without fear, and he acted as a bodyguard for others. When Joko saw his son ferrying groups of friends to and from the East end, when he saw his photo in the newspaper, watched him graduate high school and go to law school, he must have felt a rush of pride. This was what he had wanted for his family—acceptance, esteem, respect.

But there also must have been part of him that got angry over how difficult it was for immigrant families to achieve that—why they had to try so much harder to earn respect in the first place.

One day, my grandfather asked him if he ever thought about going back to visit his village. He had to be homesick, my grandfather reasoned, even if he never let on. "Wouldn't you like to go?" my grandfather asked.

Joko fixed him with a stare. "And how would I get there?"

My grandfather stumbled through an answer. Well, boat would probably be the most reasonable, he said. Maybe there was a cruise he could go on, and wouldn't a cruise be nice? He tried to explain the logistics of the vacation—where he could go, and how he could get there, and the things he could do.

But my great-grandfather unleashed a long stream of swear words, in both Croatian and Italian. Then, *"Stupido,"* he said. "I am not getting on no goddamn boat."

He would go years later, by airplane. When he returned, he climbed down onto the tarmac in Montreal and kissed the Canadian soil. If pressed about how the old country was, he only said, "It was poor when I went away, and it was poor when I went back."

As an older man, he fought to keep his license. He drove one route, and only one route, every afternoon: from the hotel to his camp across town. He put one foot on the gas pedal, one foot on the brake, and stared straight ahead. His business partner sat in the back seat, watching for traffic around him. And traffic watched for him: they could recognize his car as he cruised down the road, and they knew to get out of his way.

When he had to take his driving test over again to keep his license, that was how he showed up: One foot on the gas, one foot on the brake, his business partner in the back seat, ready for the other drivers to yield to him.

The examiner took all of this in as he settled in the front seat. "He can't be here," he said. "You can't have help on these exams."

Joko tried to explain. *No, this is how I always drive.* He tried to tell him, *It's fine.* He slid two containers across the dashboard to the examiner. First, a box of cigars. Second, because that hadn't had the desired effect, a container filled with candy.

The examiner wouldn't budge. He made the business partner

get out of the back seat. And then, not long after that, he failed Joko and revoked his license.

After everything, that is the great-grandfather story I know best. It's the incident that comes up again and again, that people love to tell when I ask about him—bribery, smokes, and sweets.

And in a strange way, it tells me how he made it in Canada. Or, if nothing else, it says more than the border crossing record, the ship manifest, or the old city directories. He was a proud man, and a strong-headed one. One who knew the value of community and family, and also knew the value of a little incentive. One who stubbornly did things his own way, even if other people didn't agree with his methods. A larger-than-life, shorter-than-passport kind of man. He lost his license, but he kept his footing in Canada.

My great-grandfather, Joko Culina, isn't that far from me. We were born less than a full century apart. I live in a house built on land that he purchased in the 1920s, and when I walk down my driveway, my feet land where his did during the Great Depression. In my kitchen, I have a ladle from the kitchen of his hotel. In the basement, I have one of his chairs that sat in the lobby—and it still holds up, although it feels like the upholstery was stuffed with wadded up paper.

In spite of that, there is so much that I don't know about him. He died before I was born, and what little I can pull together is full of holes. There are gaps in stories, missing paperwork, questions that no one posed. My grandfather always says, *No one thought to ask him.*

And then, *I wish we had.*

The Newcomers
By Rosanna Micelotta Battigelli

Part One: Sudbury, 1963
Memories & Musings

Assunta's eyes opened at the first sound. She turned her head to look at the almost four-month-old baby lying next to her on the bed, eyes still closed and tiny mouth contorting in preparation for his second, much louder cry for attention.

Was it feeding time already? Assunta felt for the clock on the night table and squinted at it in the darkened room. Almost midnight. *Just the beginning.* This baby was not like the others, allowing her the luxury of five to six hours between feedings. No, Cosimo was insatiable it seemed, with a three to four hour limit between each feeding. Around the clock. Positioning Cosimo in the crook of her arm while still lying on the bed, she whispered "Shhh" and began to nurse him and sing him a lullaby from the old country. *Ninna nanna, dormi tesor... Sleep, my treasure...*

Her thoughts always found a way back to their journey, and how they and thousands of other Italians had made the bittersweet decision to leave their impoverished homeland to seek a better life for their family overseas. Their ship was the *Saturnia*, steadfastly navigating the powerful waters of the Atlantic while she, nearing the end of her second trimester of pregnancy, spent days and nights praying to every saint imaginable that she'd survive the nausea. She had hardly been able to keep anything down.

Assunta felt the cloth scapular she always wore around her neck, bearing an image of *San Domenico Savio*. He was the protector of unborn children, and whenever she held it in her hands, she gave thanks that her daily illness on the voyage hadn't resulted in more serious consequences for her or the baby.

They had crossed the ocean like the famous explorer *Cristoforo Colombo* and were starting life in a new land—Canada. They landed in Halifax, Nova Scotia in April 1963 and arrived by train in Northern Ontario on the first of May. Almost four months after their arrival, with Nicola still searching for a steady job, and barely any understanding of English, Assunta delivered her fourth child, a son, on August 22nd. Unlike her three other children, Canada would be Cosimo's from the start.

Here they were, mid-December, and Nicola still hadn't secured steady work. How could she possibly be in the mood for Christmas? *And when exactly had she lost her spirit?* Was it when she and Nicola had realized there was no future for them working the land in southern Italy? When she had said her last goodbye to her parents, relatives and friends? When Nicola had shown her the cramped, three-room apartment in the Gatchell neighbourhood, where they would live while he tried to find work in Sudbury?

Assunta gently adjusted the position of the baby. She had to be strong. For all of them. Her eyes shifted to the two cots across the room. Under one blanket, two mounds slept soundly. Her girls, Giuseppina and Rosanna. Two-year-old Pasquale was sleeping in the corner cot.

Nicola should be back soon. He had been asked to do a two-day janitorial stint to cover for his friend Stefano, who was ill. Today was his last day and Nicola was doing a double shift. Assunta sighed. Since their arrival in Canada, her anxiety had escalated daily with Nicola's every unsuccessful attempt at finding steady work. He never had to say anything—the news was stamped on his face every evening when he walked through the door: mouth pursed in a thin line; eyebrows furrowed under clouded, disillusioned eyes; shoulders sagging. Assunta would look up expectantly when she heard the door handle turning, and seconds later, the hope in her heart would dissipate instantly as her eyes met his. Embracing him, she would hide her disappointment; it would only be an extra weight to the burden he already shouldered.

She was always thankful for the distraction the children provided. At the sound of their precious *papà's* entry, they would rush to greet him, inundating him with hugs and kisses that made him smile and seemed to resuscitate his wounded spirit. Nicola would play with them in the living room, while Assunta prepared supper—usually a simple meal of pasta and beans, or broth with bread she would bake when Cosimo was sleeping. *God help us,* she would pray silently as she cooked. *Thank you for the abundance of another meal, another day of grace. And healthy children.*

Assunta hated being in an upstairs apartment with four children. The effort of trying to keep them quiet all the time so as not to disturb the landlord and his wife, was getting to her. Between worrying every day about Nicola's job prospects, and tending to the children, her nerves were jangled.

Oh, she was grateful to the old couple for renting them the apartment. However, Assunta found herself often daydreaming about the simple dwelling she had left behind in the hamlet of Camini. She had shared it with her mother, Maria, who had lived there with her five children after her husband's death. He was 32 and she, Assunta, was only a month when he passed, succumbing to slow poisoning from buried shrapnel after serving in World War I. She had never known her father, but she would deeply miss her mother, relatives, and friends. They were close in good times and in hard times. They celebrated births and weddings at the Church of *Santa Maria Assunta*. And grieved with their neighbours when someone died, with the visitation held in the family home.

Yes, she dearly missed her hamlet of Camini, set up in the hills. *As old as the hills,* at least a thousand years, anyway, with a majestic view of the rugged limestone outcroppings, olive groves, and winding roads snaking through the countryside and leading to the Ionian Sea beyond ... Many of the towns in the province of Reggio Calabria and Sicily had been colonized by the Greeks a thousand or so years back, and were still known by their Greek names. *Placanica. Caulonia. Locri Epifeziri.*

Assunta thought of the simple stone dwelling her *mamma* still lived in, with russet roof tiles and a terrace that made you feel like you were on top of the world, looking over the distant hills and valleys to the strip of darker blue that marked the infinite stretch of the Ionian Sea. She especially longed for the pigeon soup mamma used to prepare when one of them contracted a fever. Or the huge biscotti she used to make in her wood-fired oven.

If Assunta closed her eyes, she could almost hear again the early morning commotion in the narrow streets and alleys and outlying farms: the crowing of the village roosters and the squawking of the chickens; the clicking sounds of the pigeons as they walked along the terrace; the *clip clop* of mules on the cobblestones; the melodic voices of the labourers setting out hours before dawn to go and work in the fields before the scorching Calabrian sun made it unbearable; and the laughing voices of the womenfolk, who, despite their humble circumstances and hard lives, sauntered down with wicker baskets laden with clothes on the crown of their heads to the *fontana*, the public fountains, where they could wash outdoors.

Even in the winter they went, bundled with an extra layer of clothing, to ward off the dampness that came from living so close to the Ionian Sea. The only thing that impeded them were the frequent downpours during late fall and winter. But even the coldest and dampest of Camini's winters—which produced at most one or two dustings of snow that melted soon after—could not be compared to the harsh 30 and 40 below zero winter that greeted them their first year in Sudbury. And getting about was not so easy in Sudbury. The city was much bigger and more spread out than her home town, and she wasn't about to gallivant about with four children in tow, especially not in winter.

Assunta missed the Mediterranean summers, too. Mornings spent at the *spiaggia,* the fine-pebbled beach, with other families, sharing good times despite their economic circumstances. Gathering in the *piazza* for a communal chestnut roast, laughing as their children chased after lizards or picked blackberries in the countryside, their faces smeared from all their gorging.

And the smells! The scent of oleanders with their pink or white blossoms. The scent of grapes being crushed in the fall, the aroma of tomatoes simmering in olive oil with freshly-picked oregano . . .

One of the things Assunta missed the most was the camaraderie of the villagers. There was always somebody on their balcony or doorstep, or ambling along, a terracotta jug on their head to fill at the natural spring. *Buon giorno. Salve. Buona sera.* There was a friendly voice at every turn, wishing you a good day or evening, asking about your little ones, bringing you a basket of cactus pears that they picked growing wild on the outskirts of the hamlet, rushing over to advise you with an herbal remedy if your child got sick . . .

Assunta gazed at the snowflakes spiraling downward like projectiles onto the sea of white already covering the ground. It was strange to see the land buried this way. And the trees, their leaves long gone, their branches sticking out like the skinny arms of the poorest villagers back home... There was nobody about in Gatchell at this hour, but even in the day, she hardly saw anybody.

Assunta wondered if she would ever get used to life in Canada. And the relentless cold. She was never lonely back home. But here, in this stark land, she felt the loneliness daily. Even with the children around her.

Last night, Nicola broke the devastating news to Assunta when the children were asleep. He sat on the side of the bed with her, and taking her hand, he stroked it pensively before saying quietly, "We have to move, Assunta."

Assunta's eyes widened at the implication of his words. The fact that he had uttered them so softly emphasized their gravity. She bit her lip, feeling numb, and gazed past Nicola's head to the window. Slowly she rose and walked toward it, cringing at the sound of the wooden floorboards beneath her feet. The old landlord down below was probably complaining to his wife this very minute, she thought, about the 'upstairs noise.'

She had spotted him from this window once, out in the front yard with his wife, raking up the mounds of faded oak leaves on the lawn. From the three air holes of the window, Assunta had heard him saying quite distinctly that they were a nice family, but that the children made too much noise, jumping and running around.

Shivering, she riveted her gaze back to Nicola. "Why?"

"The old man can't take the noise."

"*O Dio,* they're just being children."

"I know. But it's harder for older people. I don't like it, but I understand."

Nicola joined Assunta at the window. "Look, they're not turning us out overnight. We still have a few weeks..."

Assunta reached for a handkerchief to stem a fresh flow of tears as she recalled Nicola's words the night before. Her blurred gaze fell on the note that Nicola had left on his pillow this morning... *I didn't want to wake you, amore. Please don't worry. Today is a new day. I didn't bring you and the children to a new country to be hungry and homeless. Have faith. I'll be home around midnight. Give our beautiful bambini lots of kisses for me. Nicola.*

Assunta had made it through the day, reading Nicola's note every time a doubt or fear attempted to take root in her mind. And after Giuseppina, Rosanna and Pasquale were tucked in their beds, she lay on the bed next to Cosimo and closed her eyes, with the intent of resting a few minutes before clearing off the table and doing the dishes. When the turn of a door handle roused her from her sleep, she checked the time. Those few minutes had stretched into almost four hours. It was past midnight now.

At the sound of footsteps coming up the stairs from their apartment entrance, Assunta rose from the bed and draping a sweater over her nightgown, she tiptoed into the kitchen and turned on the light for her husband.

A moment later, Nicola was inside, his hat and coat heavily dusted with snow. Assunta walked toward him slowly, dark shadows under her eyes. Her chestnut brown hair, usually tied back during the day, was tousled, tumbling over her shoulders. Nicola gazed at her for a few seconds, the snow on his hat and coat melting along with his heart.

She stopped a foot away from him, about to give him the usual embrace, and then she froze. Nicola's mouth wasn't pursed. His eyebrows weren't drawn together. His shoulders weren't sagging. And his eyes were bright, not at all discouraged. "I found us a place," he said, smiling. "It's four blocks away from here, on Walter Street, and it's not an upstairs apartment. The landlords live on one side of the house and have four children of their own." He watched the play of emotions on Assunta's face, and then added, "My friend

169

Stefano gave my name to his foreman at the smelter in Copper Cliff. They're looking to hire. I have a meeting with him tomorrow. And tomorrow night, we're going to celebrate. Let's forget about beans and order a porketta from Albert's Meat Market. And the day after tomorrow, there's going to be a spaghetti supper in St. Anthony's Church basement. It's time we met some of our neighbours around here and made some friends, don't you think?"

Assunta was silent for a moment, and then gave a shout of elation, not caring if all the children woke up, or even if the landlord woke up and banged his cane repeatedly on the ceiling, as he was apt to do when the children made too much noise running around. She flung her sweater in the air, and Nicola, laughing, swung her around.

Assunta caught a glimpse of the snow swirling outside the window. And beyond the rooftops, the INCO stack, a beacon of hope for Nicola and for all of them. Maybe she could get used to snow, she thought, smiling. At least now, she'd have a reason to try.

Christmas 1963 was going to be the start of a new life for all them in Sudbury. Thanks to God . . . and *Cristoforo Colombo*.

Part Two: Sudbury, 1965
Doesen't *Anyone* Speak Like *Mamma?*

Rosanna looked like some of the other children in her Kindergarten class at St. Anthony's School in Gatchell. She had dark brown hair that her *Mamma* had arranged into pigtails with white ribbons. She was wearing a pretty flowered dress that *Mamma* made for her first day of school, with material she had brought with her from Italy. Her shoes looked like the shoes the other girls were wearing, all shiny and brown and new.

But Rosanna knew that she was different.

The other children were playing at activity centres and she was not. The teacher was looking down at her. Words were coming out of the teacher's mouth, but they didn't sound like *Mamma's* words.

She wished *Mamma* hadn't brought her to school. And why had she taken her sister Giuseppina to another room? Rosanna wanted to go back home, but the teacher was holding her hand and Rosanna didn't know what to say.

The teacher looked like a nice lady. She had light blonde hair with a big bun that sat on her head like a nest. She was wearing bright orange-red lipstick, a colour that reminded Rosanna of the sweet persimmons she used to eat back in Italy, the country where she was born. The teacher's eyes were blue. Blue like the sparkling Ionian Sea that Rosanna splashed in during the long, hot summer. Her family and other families would wake up early to get to the beach before 8 a.m., so they could enjoy a few hours before the blazing Calabrian sun reached its peak and made the beach sand too hot to walk on.

The teacher was talking to her again. Rosanna could tell by the sound of her voice that she was asking a question, but she had no idea what the teacher wanted to know, so she said nothing. She just bit her lip and looked down at the floor.

"Can...you...speak...English?" The teacher bent down until she was eye-to-eye with Rosanna. Her words were very loud.

Rosanna looked around. Other children walked by her, talking and laughing. One boy pointed at her and giggled. They all sounded different, just like the teacher.

Didn't *anyone* speak like *Mamma?*

Rosanna felt her eyes prickle with tears. She didn't want to cry in front of the teacher and the other children, but she didn't know if she could stop herself. She looked back at the teacher, who was still smiling, but Rosanna could not smile back. She had no words for the teacher.

She wanted to go home. She wanted to hide. *Why had her*

Mamma left her?

"Sit here, Rosanna." The teacher pointed to the large mat on the floor.

Rosanna wondered what she was trying to say. When the teacher patted the mat and made a motion for her to sit, Rosanna understood and sat down.

The teacher nodded and then walked away and Rosanna felt worse than before. She was the only child sitting on the mat. All the others were playing: some at the sandbox; some in the kitchen centre; some with blocks. Most were laughing, having fun. She saw one boy build a tall tower out of different coloured blocks, and then burst into laughter when it toppled over. Two girls in the house centre were holding up dolls to face the other, and pretending they could talk to each other. She felt like a little toad alone in a big, green field. She felt her lips tremble.

I must have done something wrong, she thought, and wished she had never come to school. *Maybe the teacher is angry because I didn't speak to her. Maybe she will make me stay on the mat all day . . . all alone . . .*

Rosanna squeezed her eyes shut. She wished she had magic powers, like the magician her *Mamma* and *Papà* took her to see at the country fair in the neighbouring hamlet of Riace before they moved to Canada. He could make a rabbit appear out of an empty hat.

Oh, if only she could do magic tricks, she would make herself disappear and then she would fly far, far away, back to the place where she was born, where people spoke the way she did. Where people spoke like her *Mamma.*

She opened her eyes and a boy with gleaming green eyes and curly red hair stuck his face in front of her and shouted "Peek-a-boo!" and then ran off, laughing. Rosanna's lip started to tremble. She had never seen red hair before. Most people had dark or light brown hair where she came from.

"*Ciao, Rosanna,*" said someone behind her.

She turned around. A girl with brown eyes and long brown hair was standing next to the teacher. The teacher was holding her hand.

"*Ciao, Rosanna,*" the girl said again, looking right at her. Her dark brown eyes were sparkling like the shiny stones Rosanna used to collect on the beach in Italy. "Hello."

Rosanna's heart thumped so loudly she wondered if others could hear it. "*Ciao,*" she replied with a shy smile.

The teacher knelt down and smiled at both of them. "This is Maria," she said to Rosanna. "She will be your friend. Your *amica.* She is *calabrese* too. She will help you to learn English."

Rosanna looked back at Maria, who was smiling and nodding. Rosanna understood only two words her teacher had said: Maria and *amica.*

Maria held out her hand to Rosanna and said, "*Andiamo a giocare,* Rosanna." And then more slowly, "Let's . . . go . . . play."

Rosanna stepped forward and took Maria's hand. She gave her teacher a bright smile.

Maybe she didn't need magic powers after all. Having a new friend who spoke like her *Mamma* was magic enough.

Waiting For The Ice To Melt
By Darlene Naponse

Non-Stop YWG – DEN

You watch the weather radar over and over. No sound while weather blobs drift through your reserve. You were not there; you wonder if he knew as the blobs encapsulate, explode and develop.

The ice has not melted off the lakes and you anticipate heat, imagining aside.

Delayed once again, everyone fixated on the usual cellular relation. Look up and back down searching till the call.

Mother Earth is still suspended. You are not cold.

Non-Stop DEN – ABQ

Faded, hungry and looking for Elsie, you stood in line and waited your turn.

Lefty, the sweet Navajo from Window Rock, now living in Denver, asked you to look out for his mother. He was scanning the area for a cousin, a Nishnaabe, Nichee, Nat, Diné, Native, Indian, Original, Indigenous anyone who looked brown and maybe from a

Rez to watch over his Mother cause that's what we do for each other.

Walking down the corridor, the sports teams occupy the wall. Their thundering appease each other cheers you up. You forget about the stained carpet and dirty concrete walls. Or the fact that every window had not been washed for months, maybe years. You wonder why this area is so unkempt. Why the area you accessed via stairs just felt so unwelcoming.

You look around and find your seat. 16D, Elsie is in 15B. She is in front of you. The man you are sitting beside immediately speaks.

"Gonna be a rough ride."

A quick nod acknowledges his fear. With a gentle touch you reach out towards Elsie. You let her know Lefty is still watching over her. She smiles. She is ninety-six years old. Her beauty is striking and invigorating. Her smile calms you. You fall into every crease of her brown skin and map out at least seven stories. Then, you have a sense of home. You left the cold white land where you were born, seven days ago. One day too long, you are starting to forget how to distinguish home and the road.

"I feel it. This might be the last ride."

He is eating skittles. He offers skittles. You nod no, then giggle 'cause you hope it is not true. You look out the window beside him. His tattooed arms are a distraction; there are so many you want to linger and look at the detail.

"Don't look so bad out there."

He sits back, grips the chair and looks out.

"Gonna be a rough one. I text my kids, told them I was sorry."

You sit back and peer towards Elsie. You wonder if she thought it was the last ride. You see no hesitation in her eyes. You touch your phone, you think about your own apologies. You think about your parents who are waiting for grandkids. You think about your

175

husband who is home. (You are gone again.) You think about your sister and how you never said thank you enough.

"No worries, here we come Albuquerque," you say.

That moment when the plane accelerates and lifts, you are in the air, there is no turning back. In silence you sit side by side. Fog drifting by, white fluff stops your sight and your breath.

Everyone is still, looking forward, waiting for a reaction from the flight attendant. You gage your fear by her calm or concern. She is a master of control. You have no idea if this flight is going to be lost in the desert or in the mountains or settled on the dream.

The plane slips, falls out of its equilibrium. It feels like it missed the last step. Then the pilot corrects and its slipstream holds you up.

The attendant, stares past you. What is she looking at? Are they talking with each other with that blank sense to try to ignore the horror?

You cannot translate nor make up any conversation they may be having. The silence makes you panic. You want to laugh just to feel the equilibrium you lost. Then you yawn. The clouds are still sparse. A blue sky is somewhere.

Elsie is comfortable. She puts her head back. You do the same 'cause you have no independence at the moment.

The plane turns, you scratch at your palm. It tickles. You are real.

"Seriously, I'm okay to go."

His fast talk confuses you. You imagine he is an ex extreme bike racer or ex ski champion. An ex, still challenging the event. Tattooed Angels are on his left arm, closest to you. You would take it as a sign, but you gave up on religion at your cousin's wedding when you were seventeen. You are supposed to respond, maybe, but you just smile.

You look at Elsie, she is relaxed. Finally the plane straightens out. The calm sinks down out the floor.

"My brother is a pilot. He always has to talk someone down," he says, while holding his phone.

"Someone always freaks out on his plane."

"My name is Hondo."

You tell him your name, but wonder more about his.

"How old are you?"

"I'm forty"

"Shit I thought you were in your twenties"

You laugh. The flattery is nice, but you wonder if your immaturity shows or is it just the family genes. Everyone looks young in your family.

"Are you married?"

"Yes for 8 years."

You only mention the eight years you are married, but don't mention the seven years before that. How you managed to make it through fifteen years.

"I was married three times."

Hondo shows you pictures of his kids. He starts with his son. He shows you a picture of him and his son. His son is jumping into the picture, he is half the size of him. His daughter is biking. She can hardly reach the pedals.

"Fun ages."

"It was. Now all they want is money."

He shows you a picture of his daughter's high school graduation.

"That is my ex."

"We were married for 11 years. We love each other but can't stand each other."

The airplane falls into what feels like a thousand feet of cotton batten. You relax your hands.

150 YEARS UP NORTH AND MORE

"We are best friends and parents. We choose that, rather than destroying everything around us."

"My daughter has a son. She is an environmental scientist. My son, is in his last year of college - engineering."

"It is all from their mother."

He sits back then moves around his chair. He looks around the plane.

"You have any kids?"

You say no.

"You should get home and get on that."

He shows me a picture of his grandson.

"My kids are the proudest thing I ever did. They got older, I get better."

"I'm buying a condo."

"I love downtown now."

"I used to live in the mountains."

Hondo scratches his day old beard.

"I live in the bush. On a reserve in Northern Ontario." You answer, 'cause you are trained to be responsive.

"Canada," you say.

"Why would you go to Albuquerque? It's a piece of shit city – full of crime and it is ugly."

"I'm heading to Santa Fe, never really seen Albuquerque."

The plane hits turbulence. Hondo pulls out his phone and texts his kids. *I love you. If I die you are rich.*

You laugh. You look around. And check up on Elsie. The sweet grandmother is sleeping.

You wonder if you can do the same. Not the kids, but sleep.

"Last night I got drunk and booked this flight to surprise my Mother for Mother's day."

He grabs his chair and stares out the window. You look down at your boots. Your feet are hot, you packed wrong again. Winnipeg was freezing. When you get home to Northern Ontario, the trees will start to bud, the ice will start to melt.

The plane hits turbulence. The stewardess walking towards you, grabs onto your chair. You lock eyes with her and express a sense of stillness with a false look.

The pilot speaks. The stewardess rushes back to her seat. Everyone is quiet.

"Hello, this is Captain James P. Kent. We are about ..."

His voice disappears.

"24000 ft. altitude"

You have no idea what he is saying.

"A little story today, we are going to drop to ..."

Some more inaudible information is shared. You lose interest quickly, like usual.

"And it will be smooth flying from there."

"It's been raining for two days. It sucks I'm in construction." Hondo adds.

Hondo checks his seatbelt, and looks out the window.

Elsie is still sleeping. Her hair has not budged, still perfectly curled. You think about home, about the water. You imagine yourself at camp, fishing, walking the land, once the ice melts.

The plane levels off again. A man gets up and walks towards the bathroom. The stewardess is about to tell him to stay seated, then the seatbelt light goes off.

You lean back, close your eyes. You listen to the plane's engine. Its deep rotation settles you. You dream about the lavender and the brushes. Unlike home you can see onward for miles in Santa Fe. The mountains feel like a pocket, holding only you.

You anticipate the warmth. You look forward to the dry earth. You just finished minus thirty degrees Celsius most of the winter. Some days were minus forty. The sun is your friend. You miss it. You want the dust and the sand.

150 YEARS UP NORTH AND MORE

You wake up; Hondo is leaning on you, asleep. The plane starts to drop. He leans back into his space. You straighten your posture to feel alive.

"Did you nap?" Hondo asks.

"Yes, it is like a new day," you answer.

Hondo looks out at the window, as we fly over the flat lands.

"It was good to nap beside you," Hondo says.

You agree with a nod and a smile.

Hondo keeps talking, while the plane shakes. The stewardess rushes to her seat, missing a step but correcting her balance as she sits. Composed she puts on her seatbelt. She hits one last button. The 351-mile flight will soon end.

"My father came to Albuquerque in his twenties. Bought property when nothing was here. He made his money buying cheap land."

"Pueblo land from the Sandia, Zia, Isleta, Santa Ana people." you reply.

" Yeah. He was an asshole. We don't talk. But I took his money."

The silver tube you fly in is starting to descend. The clouds wipe your tears you cannot produce. The plane floats throughout your mind. Turbulent – imagining falling luggage, no drink service.

A roar, a friction at your feet. Land controlled landscape, picked over, combed, mined, manicured, treated. A façade fake as cotton candy.

These the Lands of the Pueblo land from the Sandia, Zia, Isleta, Santa Ana people, sacred, learned, natural, beautiful.

When the plane stops you hear the customary belt buckles coming off and people rush to exit. You watch Elsie, she takes her time. She rises without obstruction. You help her with her bag and follow her out.

Hondo quickly exits. As he does, he turns around and smiles.

180

You smile back.

Having so many people around you brings attention to your anxieties. You prefer silence. You prefer trees.

Elsie reminds you of home. You wonder what your grandmother would have looked like if she made it past forty-five. Your face is the same shape as your grandmother's. You and Elsie walk in silence. When you get out of security and down towards luggage, Elsie looks around. She doesn't see her granddaughter. You tell her you will wait with her. The airport is humid. Your senses start to relate to the warmth.

Elsie shares a story with you about her granddaughter, the granddaughter we wait for. It ends with biting sharpness. You both laugh; laugh so hard that the flight stress disappears. The laughter reminds you that your community is beautiful, beyond the reserve-imposed boundaries.

Elsie asks if I can call her granddaughter on my cell. She is worried about her. They are only fifteen minutes late. During the conversation the granddaughter mentions there was an accident along Hwy 40, they were stuck in traffic. They are 10 minutes away from the airport.

The granddaughter tells me this, like I am from here. That's what we do, we are all cuzzins.

Elsie reminds you of your grandmother, the one you never met. Yet she appears in your dreams and your sister's dreams. She is with you all the time. Your face is shaped like hers. The one picture you have of her, you see where you get your melancholy, your reverence, your need to protect.

When they arrive, Elsie's Granddaughter, her two children and another cuzzin all walk into the airport to greet Elsie. They hug her, you feel love. They hug you and wave as they leave. Elsie is home. She is safe. Lefty, the sweet Navajo from Window Rock now living in Denver can breathe.

No one is at the shuttle counter. You forgot to book the shuttle again. You sit down and start to read. You prepare for the week ahead of you. As you start to get into the story, the employee opens the counter.

You walk outside towards the air porter. The warm New Mexico air and sun instantly falls upon you. The mountains are in the distance like you remembered. You text your husband. You make a mental note to see more of Albuquerque. It reminds you of Sudbury, the town near your reserve. All the connecting cities from reserve to reservation.

Acknowledgements

We wish to thank Waubgeshig Rice for coming on board as Indigenous editorial advisor, for his thoughtful and insightful feedback and to Verna Hardwick and Mary Anne Corbiere for their careful analysis and knowledge of the Anishinaabemowin - Ojibway language.

A heartfelt thank you to all contributors, for sharing their personal stories with such honesty and accuracy and their dedication to this project.

And lastly, to the Ontario Arts Council, and the Canada Council of the Arts for supporting Northern Ontario culture and history.

Contributor biographies

Julie-Anne Bolduc is an artist, teacher, and writer living in Sudbury.

Born in Thunder Bay, she grew up in Temiskaming Shores. She participated in Sudbury Theatre Centre's Playwright Junction and received a grant for her play. She competed in the Song of the Year Songwriting Contest placing as a runner-up three times. She also had paintings commissioned by Laurentian University and several exhibits around Sudbury.

Rod Carley is Artistic Director of Canadore College's Acting for Stage and Screen Program in North Bay and a part-time English professor at Nipissing University. He has written articles for *Borrowers and Lenders: The Journal of Shakespeare and Appropriation,* Theatre Ontario, *Highgrader Magazine* and *How to Be An Actor And Survive,* an entertainment industry guidebook. He is also an award-winning director, playwright and actor, having directed and produced over 100 theatrical productions to date including fifteen adaptations of Shakespeare.

Rod recently had principal roles on the television series *Cardinal, Hard Rock Medical* and *Carter.* He was the 2009 winner of TVO's Big Ideas/Best Lecturer competition. As a kid, Rod enjoyed flattening pennies on the tracks with his pals and counting freight train cars at railway crossings.

Rod's debut novel, *A Matter of Will,* was published by Latitude 46 Publishing in September 2017. He is currently at work on a second novel.

www.rodcarley.ca

Evelyn Clara Diebel shares a home in Nairn Centre with her high school sweetheart husband who has always been on the other end of her teeter totter. She dangles her life between being a wife, the mother of three adult sons and with the seriousness of her work, as an Adult Literacy Professor at Cambrian College in Espanola, and a Masters student. Her friends would say that she is a passionate, energetic woman who just doesn't sleep. Evelyn is always scheming to surround herself with books, food, wine, friends, music, and the beauty of nature. When she is not devoting her time to academia, or community activities, she is planning and preparing the next meal and get-together at home or at camp for family and friends.

Franca Dominelli Lisi was born in Serra San Bruno in Calabria, Italy and immigrated to Kearney, Ontario with her family at the age of five. Four years later, they settled in Sudbury.

Franca and her husband raised two children, Robert and David, who are now married with children of their own.

Franca has always wanted to write family stories, recording events as seen through the eyes of a five-year old. As immigrants, each one of us has experienced life in different ways. With the encouragement of her sons, Franca has begun her collection of stories, including *From Serra San Bruno . . . to Sudbury.*

Susan Eldridge-Vautour lives in the forest beside the Vermilion River, west of Sudbury. Writing since 2007, Susan's work has appeared in various Canadian literary magazines as well as in collections by small Canadian publishers. In 2012, she received an Ontario Arts Council Grant to complete her, yet unpublished, novel. *History of Small-handed Women* is a version of a longer piece waiting (perhaps wanting) to be written.

Kim Fahner lives and writes in Sudbury, Ontario. She was the fourth poet laureate of the City of Greater Sudbury (2016-18), and was the first woman to be appointed to the role. Kim has published four volumes of poetry, including: *You Must Imagine the Cold Here*; *braille on water*; *The Narcoleptic Madonna*; and *Some Other Sky* . Two of her plays have had staged readings at the Sudbury Theatre Centre, and one, *Sparrows Over Slag*, had a staged reading (in collaboration with Pat the Dog Theatre Creation) at Wordstock Sudbury Literary Festival, in November 2017. Kim has also completed a novel, a piece of historical fiction set in a Northern Ontario mining town, titled *The Donoghue Girl*. She is a member of the League of Canadian Poets, the Writers' Union of Canada, and PEN Canada. Kim blogs at kimfahner.wordpress.com at The Republic of Poetry, and has a website at www.kimfahner.com

Julio Heleno Gomes is a native of Portugal but has spent the majority of his life in Thunder Bay. He is a graduate of Lakehead University and has been a practising journalist for more than 25 years. In his career as a reporter and columnist, he has covered entertainment, municipal and provincial politics as well as police and court. His byline has also appeared in the *Toronto Star, London Free Press, Winnipeg Free Press and Halifax Chronicle Herald.* His recent fiction has been honoured by the Canadian Authors Association National Capital Writing Contest (NCWC) and the Northwestern Ontario Writers Workshop.

His interests include reading, writing, movies, music, theatre and sports.

Liisa Kovala is a Finnish-Canadian teacher and writer living in Sudbury, Ontario. She is a member of the Writers' Union of Canada, Canadian Authors' Association and Sudbury Writers' Guild. A graduate of University of Toronto's Creative Writing program, Liisa has published fiction and creative non-fiction pieces in several publications and anthologies, including *Chicken Soup for the Soul: The Spirit of Canada and Christmas in Canada, Along the 46th, Canadian Teacher Magazine, Creepy Capreol Junior,* and *Kiipis! Literary Journal.* Her family memoir *Surviving Stutthof: My father's memories behind the Death Gate* was published by Latitude 46 Publishing in September 2017. She is currently working on a novel.

Margo Little is a journalist, photographer and educator from Manitoulin Island. She holds an MA in Interdisciplinary Humanities from Laurentian University. She is the past Communications Officer of the B.C. Association of Friendship Centres and the author of the silver anniversary commemorative edition of *The Evolution of Friendship Centres.* Other non-fiction publications include *The Other Woman Was Lady Luck* and the *Moral Dilemma of High Stakes Gambling in Native Communities.* In addition, she has contributed to the *Journal of Aboriginal Economic Development,* the *Aboriginal Curatorial Collective Journal, Windspeaker* and *Ontario Birchbark.* As a charter member of the Sudbury Writers' Guild and founder of the Manitoulin Writers' Circle, she continues to publish literary fiction, poetry and creative non-fiction.

Caitlin Sylvia McAuliffe is a Finnish, Irish and Dutch northern Ontarian who grew up in Whitefish, Ontario and spent weekends on Lake Panache. Currently completing a Women's Studies, Indigenous Studies and Sociology Degree at Laurentian University in Sudbury, she is also an Artist at Woodland Sisters with Cassidy Jean McAuliffe. She lives in Whitefish, Ontario.

Sarah McComb lives and breathes the written word, with a certificate in Creative Book Publishing from Humber College and a job at the public library to prove it. Her writing has previously appeared in publications by several organizations, including the Ontario Poetry Society, White Mountain Publications, and the Writers' Community of Durham Region. She is a recent transplant to Sault Ste. Marie, Ontario, where she loves having the opportunity to research her family's history in the city. She never had a chance to meet her great-grandfather but would like to think she can see a bit of his stubbornness in herself.

Rosanna Micelotta Battigelli is a charter member and past president of the Sudbury Writers' Guild. She is also an alumna of The Humber School for Writers, and her fiction has appeared in over a dozen Canadian anthologies, including *Along the 46th* and *A Second Coming: Canadian Migration Fiction.* Her latest stories appear in *Chicken Soup for the Soul: Inspiration for Teachers* and in *VIA's* (Voices in Italian Americana) special issue dedicated to contemporary Italian folktales. Rosanna's novel *La Brigantessa,* awarded an Ontario Arts Council Writers' Works in Progress Grant, will be published by Toronto's Inanna Publications in 2018.

William R. Morin is an educator, artist and cultural consultant. He is of Ojibway / Scottish / French Canadian ancestry, a member of the Michipicoten First Nation, where he lives and works in northern Ontario with his Anishinaabe-Kwe wife Robin and their 4 children. Will is an accomplished and award winning visual artist exhibiting nationally. Will has toured nationally and internationally as a traditional. Working in all media, Will is also an accomplished spoken word artist, traditional Anishinaabek storyteller, actor (founding member of Theatre Cambrian), modern dancer (Earth Dancer with Sudbury School of Dance) and an avid poet. He is a multi-disciplined academic with 3 bachelor's degrees, an Interdisciplinary Masters , presently working on an

Interdisciplinary Human Studies PhD. Will has taught for over 20 years from elementary to post secondary, currently Indigenous Studies for 19 years at the University of Sudbury / Laurentian University. Will served in the Canadian Armed Forces during the first Gulf War trained as a Medical Assistant.

Darlene Naponse is an Anishinaabe from Atikameksheng Anishnawbek – northern Ontario, where she was born and raised. She is a writer, independent film director, video artist and community activist. She completed her MFA in Creative Writing at the Institute of American Indian Arts (IAIA) in Santa Fe. Several of her short stories have been published in the *Yellow Medicine Review, Along the 46th* and the *Malahat Review*. She was a 2017 Writers' Trust/McClelland & Stewart Journey Prize Finalist for her short story *She is Water*.

Darlene is currently working on a book of short stories. She works from her studio on the Rez (Atikameksheng Anishnawbek).

Shawna Diane Partridge was born and raised in Sault Ste. Marie, Ontario. She earned a Liberal Studies Diploma from Sault College and a Bachelor of Arts Honours in English from Laurentian University.

She later pursued a Master of Arts in English Language and Literature at Queen's University and then a Master of Arts in Creative Writing at the University of Windsor. She has worked as Managing Editor of *Rampike* magazine and Editorial Assistant for the *Windsor Review: An International Journal of Life, Literature and Art*. She has spoken and/or performed at Wordstock Sudbury Literary Festival; Le Salon du livre du Grand Sudbury; BookFest Windsor; and "Women of Words Unite: in conversation about the power of words", an event of her own planning.

Her first book, *Rule of Seconds*, was published by Latitude 46

Publishing in May 2016. It was shortlisted for a Northern Lit Award: Fiction Category. Residing in Sudbury, Shawna is currently writing the sequel to *Rule of Seconds*. She is a proud member of The Writers' Union of Canada.

Hussein Qarqouz is a baker and entrepreneur originally from Syria who now lives in Sudbury.

Hussein and his family arrived in Sudbury in late 2015 as part of Citizenship and Immigration Canada's Private Sponsorship of Refugees Program.

Hussein, along with his wife Sawsan and their three boys, Mohammad, Ousama and Nabil were sponsored for refugee resettlement by St. Andrew's United Church.

Hussein's father Mohammad joined the family one month later. Their fourth son Omar was born in 2016, a Canadian citizen.

Hussein and his wife Sawsan are planning to open Damascus Coffee and Bakery in 2018.

Lee Weimer grew up in the northern Ontario bush country, surrounded by spruce and muskeg, moulding her experience of life. She had no other choice but to become familiar with earth, wind and sky. She says the land we walk on takes hold of you and never lets you go.

This is her first short story. Lee never thought she would be able to do it. And now she's thinking of writing a book of short stories. Life can be amazing that way.

Editor biographies

Karen McCauley is a storyteller and Assistant Professor at Laurentian University's School of Social Work. She has a life-long interest in stories of identity, and employs narrative techniques and literary approaches, including memoir and autobiography to teach contemporary issues in social work practice, policy making and administration. Karen seeks out and attempts to co-create forums where individual and community stories can be disseminated and used to help advance greater equality and positive social change. She was a contributing author to *Along the 46th*, twice shortlisted for *Briar Patch* magazine's annual Writing in the Margins creative short fiction competition, in addition to a number of academic publications.

Laura Stradiotto is co-founder of Latitude 46 Publishing, and a writer and journalist who has written for publications across Canada and the U.S., covering a broad range of topics from arts and culture to parenting, social justice and women's rights. In the area of content development and marketing, she has worked for a broad range of clients and platforms, both public and private sector, and across diverse sectors, including mining, tourism and business. She has an MFA in Creative Non Fiction from the University of King's College in Halifax, N.S.